IMPROVE YOUR BIDDING AND PLAY

Derek Rimington
& Ron Klinger

CASSELL
IN ASSOCIATION WITH
PETER CRAWLEY

First edition published 1999
This new enlarged edition published 2002
Second impression 2004
in association with Peter Crawley
by Cassell
Wellington House, 125 Strand, London, WC2R 0BB
a member of the Orion Publishing Group

A catalogue record for this book
is available from the British Library

ISBN 0 304 36330 8

Typeset in Australia by Modern Bridge,
Northbridge, NSW 1560, Australia

Printed in Great Britain by
Mackays of Chatham, Kent

Acknowledgement

The authors acknowledge with appreciation
the assistance of Len Dixon of Canberra
who has made many valuable suggestions
which have been implemented in this edition.

CONTENTS

IMPROVE YOUR BIDDING AND PLAY
new edition

Here is the review of the first edition of *Improve Your Bidding and Play* published in the prestigious *Bridge Magazine:*

'This book is a treasure trove for players who want to improve. As well as containing some interesting hands from the past it will do exactly what it says. If you play standard, modern Acol this is a book you simply must buy now, if not for yourself but for your partner. It adopts the standard quiz format so that each hand is analysed first as a bidding problem, where modern methods are discussed in a constructive manner, and then on the second page as a real play problem. The answer will not be to find some exotic squeeze or bizarre esoteric unblocking play but will be a sound application of the basic technical principles.

So, if you really want to improve your play and your partner's bidding, buy this book and work steadily through it a couple of pages a night. There are plenty of bidding issues raised – not weird conventions that never come up but modern treatments and the principles behind them – which you could then discuss with your partner and it will pay dividends.

What is more, this book is no dry textbook but it is written in a conversational style making it almost too good a read; it tempts you to rush through it rather than give each point raised the attention it deserves. This is a book that all aspiring players should read.'

In this new edition Derek Rimington, British captain, international player, author, leading journalist and teacher, and Ron Klinger, world-famous bridge writer, teacher and an international player, have made some updating revisions and have added a further sixteen pages of new problems.

INTRODUCTION

This book is designed to test and improve both your bidding and your declarer play. Each problem begins by showing your hand and asking a question about what you would bid at that particular stage of the auction. The bidding then progresses and you are asked to choose your next action. Finally, you are given your hand and partner's as a single dummy problem. The contract and the lead are stated and you are then asked to plan the play. Occasionally the play has progressed two or three tricks before you gain the lead and have to decide how to continue to best advantage.

As a learning aid, it is hard to do better than the quiz approach but the benefits will be lost if you peek at the answer before you have made your own decision. For the play section, this is managed by having each solution overleaf, but as the bidding questions and answers for each problem all occur on the one page, it is useful to take some measures to conceal the answers. To this end, use an opaque sheet of paper or cardboard and as you tackle a problem, cover everything below the first question. After you have your answer ready, move the sheet down to reveal the answer and the next question, but not further. Again, after you have your next answer, move the sheet down to the next question or remove the sheet and study the play problem if there are no more questions about the auction.

The system in use is standard, modern Acol bidding four-card suits, a 12-14 1NT opening and a 20-22 2NT. For slam bidding, cue-bidding and Roman Key Card Blackwood are used. From time to time, suggestions are made as to how your bidding structure might be improved. Naturally, you are free to adopt or reject these suggestions. If you are ever likely to play against the authors in any tournament, we would prefer you to reject our suggestions and not use them against us.

Some of the hands occurred in match play and may therefore have been seen before but now it is possible to expand the explanations both for the bidding and the play. A few of these problems have been modified so that even if you think you recognise the problem, test yourself on it again. Perhaps something has been changed to provide a different perspective and a new answer.

Where the hands have an historical background, the details are provided. On most of the hands, the names have been omitted to protect the guilty (those who did not find the best line at the table).

You will find no squeezes or exotic plays in this book. The problems are all of the bread-and-butter variety, practical situations which occur again and again. Those who win at bridge do so less by brilliant technique and more by avoiding blunders or inferior plays in the everyday situations. Each of the play solutions carries with it the logic behind the approach adopted. That is what we hope you will absorb, the reasoning that propels you to the best line of play each time.

Importantly, for every play problem, you are required to make your contract as safely as possible or to give yourself the best chance for success. Do not concern yourself at all with overtricks or the number of undertricks. Make the contract — that is your mission.

You, the reader, have a distinct advantage over the original declarers. At the table, no one is ringing alarm bells that declarer should take particular care. In quiz form you are forewarned and know that there must be a technical point. Therefore be on the *qui vive* but enjoy yourself and hopefully raise your own standard of bridge.

Derek Rimington
Ron Klinger
1999, 2002

1. You, West, hold:

♠ 8 5 2	Dealer West : Both vulnerable			
♡ A Q 8 7 4	WEST	NORTH	EAST	SOUTH
◇ Q 6	1♡	No	2♣	No
♣ K Q 7	?			

What action should West take?

Answer: The basic choices are 2♡ and 3♣. Partner is entitled to expect 4-card support for 3♣ but your strong three-card holding is more than adequate. 2♡ shows your 5-card suit but 3♣ shows the five hearts *and* the club support, too. It is better to show more of your hand than less. As you would open 1♣ when 4-4 in hearts and clubs and the 3♣ raise implies 4-card support, partner should deduce that you hold five hearts.

♠ 8 5 2	WEST	NORTH	EAST	SOUTH
♡ A Q 8 7 4	1♡	No	2♣	No
◇ Q 6	3♣	No	3♡	No
♣ K Q 7	?			

What do you expect from 3 ♡? Is it forcing? What next?

Answer: 3♡ is not forcing. It shows around 10-12 points and invites game. You have only 13 HCP which suggests a pass but the good club fit is encouraging. When faced with a close decision, take the action with the bigger reward if successful.

♠ 8 5 2		♠ A 7 3
♡ A Q 8 7 4	N	♡ J 10 5
◇ Q 6	W E	◇ J 5
♣ K Q 7	S	♣ A J 9 5 2

Against your 4♡, North cashes the ace and king of diamonds and shifts to the jack of spades. You win with dummy's ace and lead the jack of hearts: 2 – 4 – 3. Next comes the 10 of hearts: king – ace – North discards the ◇4.

How should West continue?

```
                    ♠ J 10 9 4
                    ♡ 3
                    ◇ A K 10 4
                    ♣ 10 8 6 4
  ♠ 8 5 2                              ♠ A 7 3
  ♡ A Q 8 7 4          N              ♡ J 10 5
  ◇ Q 6                               ◇ J 5
  ♣ K Q 7        W         E          ♣ A J 9 5 2
                         S
                    ♠ K Q 6
                    ♡ K 9 6 2
                    ◇ 9 8 7 3 2
                    ♣ 3
```

WEST	NORTH	EAST	SOUTH
1♡	No	2♣	No
3♣	No	3♡	No
4♡	No	No	No

North starts with the ace and king of diamonds and shifts to the jack of spades. You take the ace and run the heart jack. If the king is offside, you will go two down but the chance has to be taken. South, unable to gain by covering the first of dummy's honours, plays low and the jack wins. When the ♡10 is led, South covers and West wins.

As South has ♡9-6 left, West now needs to enter dummy in order to finesse the ♡8. To lead the ♣7 to the jack would spell defeat because of the 4-1 break in clubs. You can pick up South's trumps but not use dummy's extra clubs to discard your spades. The right move is to lead the king (or queen) of clubs and overtake it with the ace. If the clubs are 3-2, this cannot cost.

The ♡5 is led and the ♡8 played when South follows low. The outstanding trump is drawn and the queen of clubs cashed. When South shows out, you lead the ♣7 and finesse dummy's nine. Dummy's club winners are cashed and you discard your spade losers, thus scoring an overtrick.

2. You, West, hold:

```
♠ 7 2          Dealer East : Both vulnerable
♡ A Q J 10 9   WEST    NORTH   EAST    SOUTH
◇ A 10 7 6 3                   1♣      No
♣ A            ?
```

What action should West take?

Answer: The basic choices are 1♡ or 2♡. With a two-suiter, it is best not to start with a jump-shift.

```
♠ 7 2          WEST    NORTH   EAST    SOUTH
♡ A Q J 10 9                   1♣      No
◇ A 10 7 6 3   1♡      No      2♣      No
♣ A            ?
```

How should West continue?

Answer: Best is 2◇, new suit forcing. A jump to 3◇ is reasonable but unnecesary. It would be poor to repeat the hearts.

```
♠ 7 2          WEST    NORTH   EAST    SOUTH
♡ A Q J 10 9                   1♣      No
◇ A 10 7 6 3   1♡      No      2♣      No
♣ A            2◇      No      3♡      No
               ?
```

What do you make of 3♡? What next?

Answer: 3♡ shows 3-card support and a good hand within the context of the 2♣ rebid. Slam is likely if partner has spade control. To check on that, continue with a cue-bid of 4♣.

```
♠ 7 2                      ♠ A Q
♡ A Q J 10 9      N        ♡ K 3 2
◇ A 10 7 6 3   W     E     ◇ K 4
♣ A               S        ♣ Q 10 8 7 5 4
```

You have reached 6♡ and North leads the jack of spades. How should declarer plan the play?

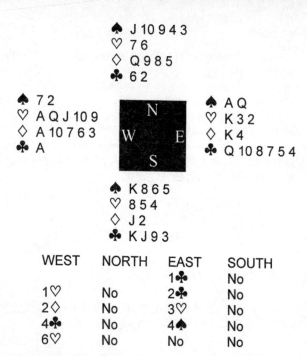

```
                    ♠ J 10 9 4 3
                    ♡ 7 6
                    ◇ Q 9 8 5
                    ♣ 6 2
  ♠ 7 2                                ♠ A Q
  ♡ A Q J 10 9           N            ♡ K 3 2
  ◇ A 10 7 6 3       W       E        ◇ K 4
  ♣ A                    S            ♣ Q 10 8 7 5 4
                    ♠ K 8 6 5
                    ♡ 8 5 4
                    ◇ J 2
                    ♣ K J 9 3
```

WEST	NORTH	EAST	SOUTH
		1♣	No
1♡	No	2♣	No
2◇	No	3♡	No
4♣	No	4♠	No
6♡	No	No	No

Once East shows spade control with the 4♠ cue-bid, West knows enough to jump to the small slam. Facing a minimum opening, West judges that a grand slam is unlikely.

To succeed, diamonds need to be established. As the most common diamond split is 4-2, you may need to ruff diamonds twice but to ruff a diamond with one of dummy's low trumps risks an over-ruff. A better move is to transfer one of the diamond ruffs to a spade ruff.

Take the ace of spades (given the spade jack lead, the king of spades is probably with South) and cash the king and ace of diamonds without touching trumps yet. Play a third diamond and ruff it with the king of hearts.

If diamonds are 3-3, draw trumps and claim. If not, cross to hand with a club and play a fourth diamond. Instead of ruffing, discard the queen of spades. This sets up your fifth diamond as a winner and you can ruff your spade loser in dummy later before drawing trumps.

3. You, West, hold:

♠ A K 2
♡ A K Q 10 9 7
◇ A K 7 4
♣ - - -

Dealer West : Both vulnerable

What action should West take as dealer?

Answer: The expectancy for a 2♣ opening is 23 HCP or more, but you may also open 2♣ below 23 HCP with three losers or fewer. When counting losers, consider only the first three rounds of each suit.

♠ A K 2
♡ A K Q 10 9 7
◇ A K 7 4
♣ - - -

Dealer West : Both vulnerable

WEST	NORTH	EAST	SOUTH
2♣	No	2NT	No
?			

What does 2NT indicate? How should West continue?

Answer: 2NT shows 8+ HCP and a balanced hand. It is sufficient to bid 3♡ at this point, as partner's hand can be very strong.

♠ A K 2
♡ A K Q 10 9 7
◇ A K 7 4
♣ - - -

WEST	NORTH	EAST	SOUTH
2♣	No	2NT	No
3♡	No	4♡	No
?			

What do you make of 4 ♡? What next?

Answer: 4♡ shows three or four hearts and leaves you as the strong hand to make the further running.

♠ A K 2
♡ A K Q 10 9 7
◇ A K 7 4
♣ - - -

♠ Q 10 6
♡ 6 5 3
◇ J 6 5 2
♣ K Q 10

Against 6♡, North leads ◇3. You play low from dummy since all is well if North has the ◇Q. You win in hand and draw trumps in three rounds, South discarding ♣2 and ♣4. When you cash the ◇K, North discards the ♣3. Is there any hope for the slam?

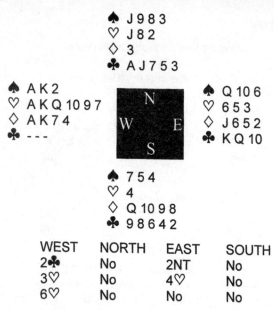

```
                ♠ J 9 8 3
                ♡ J 8 2
                ◇ 3
                ♣ A J 7 5 3

♠ A K 2            N          ♠ Q 10 6
♡ A K Q 10 9 7                ♡ 6 5 3
◇ A K 7 4      W       E      ◇ J 6 5 2
♣ - - -                       ♣ K Q 10
                   S
                ♠ 7 5 4
                ♡ 4
                ◇ Q 10 9 8
                ♣ 9 8 6 4 2
```

WEST	NORTH	EAST	SOUTH
2♣	No	2NT	No
3♡	No	4♡	No
6♡	No	No	No

A grand slam could be there but you cannot tell since you cannot discover whether East has third-round diamond control. As you should not jeopardise a good small slam for a grand slam of unknown quality, it is best simply to jump to 6♡ over 4♡.

West wins the diamond lead and draws trumps in three rounds. West cashes the second diamond winner (as a 3-2 break or the ◇Q with North will see the slam home) only to learn that the road to success is not paved with diamonds.

West needs a way to dispose of the diamond losers. The only chance is to find North with both the jack of spades and the ace of clubs. The hope is slim but there is no other.

Continue by cashing the ♠A, followed by the ♠2, finessing the ten when North follows low. When the ♠10 wins, lead the king of clubs. When South follows low, discard your ♠K.

If North takes the ♣A, he has to return a black suit which is won in dummy and you can ditch both diamond losers. If the ♣K wins the trick, simply discard a diamond on the ♠Q.

If North plays the ♠J on the second round of spades, that does nothing to hamper your plans in this case.

4. You, West, hold:

♠ 8	Dealer West : Nil vulnerable			
♡ A 5 3	WEST	NORTH	EAST	SOUTH
◇ K J 9 4 2	1◇	No	1♠	No
♣ K Q 9 2	2♣	No	2♡	No
	?			

What does 2♡ indicate? How should West continue?

Answer: 2♡ is fourth-suit-forcing, asking West to describe strength and shape further. West should rebid 2NT confirming a stopper in hearts and indicating a minimum opening.

♠ 8	WEST	NORTH	EAST	SOUTH
♡ A 5 3	1◇	No	1♠	No
◇ K J 9 4 2	2♣	No	2♡	No
♣ K Q 9 2	2NT	No	3◇	No
	3♡	No	4♣	No
	?			

Was 3◇ forcing? What did 3♡ and 4♣ mean? What next?

Answer: After fourth-suit, a bid by responder is game-forcing. As East did not pursue no-trumps, East is interested in slam in diamonds. 3♡ and 4♣ were cue-bids, showing the ace in the suit bid. 4♣ also denied the ♠A, as 3♠ was bypassed.

You should continue by asking for aces, preferably with Roman Key Card Blackwood if you use that convention. When partner bids 5♠ to show two aces and the queen of trumps, you end the bidding with 6◇.

♠ 8		♠ K 6 3 2
♡ A 5 3		♡ K 8 2
◇ K J 9 4 2		◇ A Q 10
♣ K Q 9 2		♣ A J 4

Against 6◇, North leads the ♡Q. You win in hand and, hoping for the ♠A with North, you lead the ♠8 to the king. South takes this with the ace and returns the ♡9. How do you proceed?

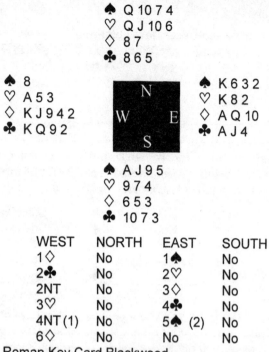

```
              ♠ Q 10 7 4
              ♡ Q J 10 6
              ◇ 8 7
              ♣ 8 6 5

♠ 8                          ♠ K 6 3 2
♡ A 5 3          N           ♡ K 8 2
◇ K J 9 4 2   W    E         ◇ A Q 10
♣ K Q 9 2         S          ♣ A J 4

              ♠ A J 9 5
              ♡ 9 7 4
              ◇ 6 5 3
              ♣ 10 7 3
```

WEST	NORTH	EAST	SOUTH
1◇	No	1♠	No
2♣	No	2♡	No
2NT	No	3◇	No
3♡	No	4♣	No
4NT (1)	No	5♠ (2)	No
6◇	No	No	No

(1) Roman Key Card Blackwood
(2) Two key cards (◇A and ♣A) plus the queen of trumps

After ♡Q to the ace, you lead the ♠8 to the king, for if North has the ♠A, you are home. When South captures the king and returns a heart, you win in dummy and your best hope now is a dummy reversal.

Ruff a spade high in hand and play a club to dummy's ace, followed by another spade ruff with a high trump.

Play a low diamond to dummy, ruff dummy's last spade with a top trump, cross to dummy with a trump and draw the missing trump, on which you discard your heart loser. Then cash clubs.

If trumps are 4-1 you will fail but it is riskier to draw two rounds of trumps before embarking on the dummy reversal plan. If either opponent began with three spades and two clubs (or even fewer black cards) a club discard on the fourth spade could lead to a club ruff before you can draw the last trump.

5. You, West, hold:

♠ K 4 2	Dealer West : Nil vulnerable			
♡ A K 9 5	**WEST**	**NORTH**	**EAST**	**SOUTH**
◇ A K Q 8 7	1◇	No	1NT	No
♣ 9	?			

What should West bid now?

Answer: You are strong enough for a jump-shift but it is enough to reverse with 2♡, which is forcing. To jump-shift would remove the bidding space vital to describe your shape.

♠ K 4 2	**WEST**	**NORTH**	**EAST**	**SOUTH**
♡ A K 9 5	1◇	No	1NT	No
◇ A K Q 8 7	2♡	No	3◇	No
♣ 9	?			

And what now?

Answer: East's 3◇ is weak and not forcing. With 16-17 points, you would pass but with 19, you should make one more effort for game. Best is to round off your shape with 3♠, simultaneously indicating your shortage in clubs.

♠ K 4 2	**WEST**	**NORTH**	**EAST**	**SOUTH**
♡ A K 9 5	1◇	No	1NT	No
◇ A K Q 8 7	2♡	No	3◇	No
♣ 9	3♠	No	4♡	No
	?			

What do you make of 4 ♡? What action do you take?

Answer: 4♡ shows 3-card support and offers the option to play in your 4-3 fit. You should reject that and remove 4♡ to 5◇.

♠ K 4 2		♠ A 8 5
♡ A K 9 5		♡ Q 6 2
◇ A K Q 8 7		◇ J 10 4
♣ 9		♣ 7 6 4 3

Against 5◇, North leads the ♠Q. How would you plan the play?

```
              ♠ Q J 9 6
              ♡ J 7 4 3
              ◇ 5 2
              ♣ A Q 10
♠ K 4 2                        ♠ A 8 5
♡ A K 9 5         N            ♡ Q 6 2
◇ A K Q 8 7    W     E         ◇ J 10 4
♣ 9               S            ♣ 7 6 4 3
              ♠ 10 7 3
              ♡ 10 8
              ◇ 9 6 3
              ♣ K J 8 5 2
```

WEST	NORTH	EAST	SOUTH
1◇	No	1NT	No
2♡	No	3◇	No
3♠	No	4♡	No
5◇	No	No	No

You have ten tricks on top and the eleventh can come from a
3-3 break in hearts or by ruffing the fourth round of hearts in
dummy if the same opponent is long in both red suits.

After winning the ♠Q with dummy's ace, cash the jack of
diamonds followed by the ◇4 to your ace. When all follow, you
cash the ace of hearts and lead a heart to dummy's queen.

When the third round of hearts is led from dummy, a third
chance emerges. When hearts break 4-2 with South holding
the doubleton, you are still all right after trumps are 3-2.

What can South do? If South ruffs the loser, you follow low.
Later you discard a spade from dummy on the ♡K and ruff a
spade in dummy. If South discards on the third heart, you take
your king and ruff your fourth heart with dummy's ◇10.

Had the defenders started by leading two rounds of clubs, a
dummy reversal is an attractive choice. You ruff the second
club, play the ◇A and a diamond to dummy. When trumps are
3-2, ruff another club, cross to the ♡Q and ruff dummy's last
club. A spade to dummy allows you to draw the last trump.

6. You, East, hold:

♠ A K J 10
♡ 9 8 4 2
◇ K 6
♣ A 7 3

Dealer West : Nil vulnerable

WEST	NORTH	EAST	SOUTH
1◇	No	?	

What should East respond?

Answer: With four-card suits it is normal to bid up-the-line but it is unwise to introduce a weak suit with a strong hand. If opener is not strong enough to reverse with 2♡, slam in hearts is unlikely. Over a 1NT rebid, you can use 2♣ Checkback to discover whether opener has four hearts. Over a 2◇ rebid, you can bid 2♡. If you receive preference for spades, the 4-3 spade fit may well be best since your trumps are so powerful.

♠ A K J 10
♡ 9 8 4 2
◇ K 6
♣ A 7 3

WEST	NORTH	EAST	SOUTH
1◇	No	1♠	No
3◇	No	?	

And now?

Answer: Slam in diamonds is likely but the hearts may be unguarded. It is risky to jump to 4NT now since the opponents may be able to take the first two or three tricks in hearts. Raise West to 4◇ to set the trump suit. In strong non-competitive sequences, raising a minor to the four-level is forcing to game and suggests slam possibilities. If partner can cue-bid 4♡ to show the control there, you can follow up with 4NT if you wish or simply jump to 6◇.

♠ 8 6   ♠ A K J 10
♡ A J   ♡ 9 8 4 2
◇ A Q J 10 8 4 ◇ K 6
♣ K 8 2   ♣ A 7 3

Against 6◇, North leads the ♡K. How should West play?

```
                    ♠ Q 9 3 2
                    ♡ K Q 10 3
                    ◇ 7 5 2
                    ♣ 6 5
  ♠ 8 6                                    ♠ A K J 10
  ♡ A J                        N           ♡ 9 8 4 2
  ◇ A Q J 10 8 4          W         E      ◇ K 6
  ♣ K 8 2                        S         ♣ A 7 3
                    ♠ 7 5 4
                    ♡ 7 6 5
                    ◇ 9 3
                    ♣ Q J 10 9 4
```

WEST	NORTH	EAST	SOUTH
1◇	No	1♠	No
3◇	No	4◇	No
4♡	No	4NT	No
5♣	No	5NT	No
6◇	No	No	No

The 5♣ reply to Roman Key Card Blackwood showed two
key cards (the red aces) plus the trump queen. 5NT confirmed
that no key cards were missing, invited a grand slam and
asked for kings. With nothing to spare, West shows one king
and 6◇ is reached, but if West held say the ♣Q instead of the
♡J, 7NT would be laydown.

After the ♡K lead, your heart loser has become exposed.
The contract is 100% safe by means of a loser-on-loser play.
Draw trumps and cash ♠A, ♠K. Continue with the jack of
spades, on which you throw the heart jack. If the ♠J wins the
trick you are home, while if North takes with the spade queen,
you discard your club loser on dummy's ten of spades later.

If East-West reach an adventurous 7◇, you need four tricks
from the spades. The best chance is to win ♡A, draw trumps
and take a first-round finesse in spades. When that wins, come
to hand in clubs, repeat the spade finesse and apologise to the
opponents with as much sincerity as you can muster.

7. You, West, hold:

♠ A 9 8 7 2   Dealer West : Both vulnerable
♡ K Q J 8 4   WEST   NORTH   EAST   SOUTH
♢ 6   ?
♣ 7 3

What should West do as dealer?

Answer: You have only 10 HCP but to pass would be a losing strategy. It pays to open 5-5 and 6-5 patterns with fewer than the basic 12 HCP. It is safer to open than to pass and enter the auction later. This is a sensible guide: Count your HCP and add 1 point for each card beyond four cards in a suit. If your hand contains a singleton or a void, open if you have 12 total points on this assessment. The above hand measures 12 on that scale and so you should open with 1♠, the higher of two five-card suits.

For this approach, a singleton ace counts full value but for other singletons, your 12 points must be outside the singleton.

♠ A 9 8 7 2   WEST   NORTH   EAST   SOUTH
♡ K Q J 8 4   1♠   No   3♠   No
♢ 6   ?
♣ 7 3

What should West do now?

Answer: A major suit opener who holds a singleton should always accept a limit raise. Bid 4♠. Yes, your hand was a minimum opening but has improved immensely after partner's 4+ raise. In loser count, you have only six losers and partner's limit raise is expected to hold three winners, thus reducing your losers to three.

♠ A 9 8 7 2   ♠ K Q 6 3
♡ K Q J 8 4   ♡ A 6 2
♢ 6   ♢ 10 5
♣ 7 3   ♣ Q 9 5 2

Against 4♠, North leads the ♢4 to South's ace and a diamond is returned. How would you plan the play?

```
              ♠ J 10 5 4
              ♡ 9 3
              ◇ K 8 7 4 3
              ♣ K J
  ♠ A 9 8 7 2                    ♠ K Q 6 3
  ♡ K Q J 8 4                    ♡ A 6 2
  ◇ 6                            ◇ 10 5
  ♣ 7 3                          ♣ Q 9 5 2
              ♠ - - -
              ♡ 10 7 5
              ◇ A Q J 9 2
              ♣ A 10 8 6 4
```

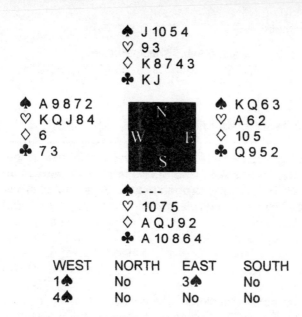

WEST	NORTH	EAST	SOUTH
1♠	No	3♠	No
4♠	No	No	No

There are only three obvious losers. When everything is easy
on normal breaks, check out the possible bad breaks. What
could go wrong? What can I do about it?

The bad news might be a 4-0 trump split or 5-0 in hearts. You
must attend to the trumps first. If they divide 2-2 or 3-1, you
can ruff a heart in dummy if necessary.

If the spades do break 4-0, you cannot avoid a loser if South
has all four trumps. No point worrying about that.

When North has the four spades, you can deal with it but it is
vital to start by cashing ♠A. If all follow, claim. If South shows
out, lead a low spade and cover North's card. If it is an honour,
return to hand in hearts and lead another trump, again simply
covering North's card. Draw the last trump and cash the hearts.

Declarer is likely to fail if the defenders start on clubs early,
but that is an improbable scenario.

Note how West's opening has paid off. North-South can make
5◇ and would no doubt have found it had West passed initially.
On the actual auction South needed to bid 3NT (the unusual
no-trump for the minors) in order to reach 5◇. Such boldness
would have paid off and is a sensible stroke with the spade void.

8. You, West, hold:

```
♠ A Q 2          Dealer West : Nil vulnerable
♡ A Q            WEST    NORTH    EAST    SOUTH
◇ J 10 7 5       ?
♣ Q J 10 2
```

What should you open as West?

Answer: Playing a 12-14 1NT opening, balanced hands in the 15-16 range start with a suit opening and rebid in no-trumps at the cheapest level. With two four-card suits, standard practice is to open the cheaper suit. On that basis, West opens 1♣.

```
♠ A Q 2          WEST    NORTH    EAST    SOUTH
♡ A Q            1♣      No       1◇      No
◇ J 10 7 5       ?
♣ Q J 10 2
```

What should West do now?

Answer: With a choice between 1NT and supporting partner, the raise is almost always best. This does not eliminate no-trumps but hiding your support may miss a slam. As you are strong, bid 3◇.

```
♠ A Q 2          WEST    NORTH    EAST    SOUTH
♡ A Q            1♣      No       1◇      No
◇ J 10 7 5       3◇      No       3♠      No
♣ Q J 10 2       ?
```

What now?

Answer: 3♠ shows a stopper in spades and asks you to bid 3NT with strength in the unbid suit. Your hearts are strong. Bid 3NT.

```
♠ A Q 2                        ♠ K J 9
♡ A Q                          ♡ 7 6 4
◇ J 10 7 5                     ◇ K Q 4 2
♣ Q J 10 2                     ♣ K 8 3
```

Against 3NT, North leads ♡3, South playing ♡K. Plan the play.

```
              ♠ 8 5 3
              ♡ J 9 8 3 2
              ◇ 9 3
              ♣ A 7 4

♠ A Q 2              N          ♠ K J 9
♡ A Q                          ♡ 7 6 4
◇ J 10 7 5      W       E      ◇ K Q 4 2
♣ Q J 10 2           S         ♣ K 8 3

              ♠ 10 7 6 4
              ♡ K 10 5
              ◇ A 8 6
              ♣ 9 6 5
```

WEST	NORTH	EAST	SOUTH
1♣	No	1◇	No
3◇	No	3♠	No
3NT	No	No	No

With the ♡K with South, 5◇ would be laydown barring a defensive ruff. There is no point crying over spilt milk. That is history. Focus on the task at hand, giving yourself the best chance to make 3NT.

You have five winners in the majors and need four from the minors. If the hearts are 4-4, there will be no problem. If they are 5-3 or 6-2, the defence can prevail. You know that but the defenders do not. The best hope is to sneak a trick in one of the minors and having done that, set up three in the other.

The most promising subterfuge is to lead the jack of clubs, a 'pretend-finesse'. If North has the ♣A and plays second hand low, you shift to diamonds at trick 3. Note that it may not be safe for North to grab the ace of clubs. If declarer began with ♡A-Q-10, another heart from North would be expensive, while if South does come in with the ♣Q, a heart through declarer's Q-10 would be ideal for the defence.

If declarer expected South to hold the ♣A, the best chance would be to cross to dummy in spades and lead a low club, but there is no reason here to place South with the club ace.

9. You, West, hold:

♠ A Q J 9 5   Dealer West : Both vulnerable
♡ A K 6   WEST   NORTH   EAST   SOUTH
◇ K Q J   ?
♣ 9 5

What should West open?

Answer: To open 1♠ risks partner passing when game may be a respectable contract. An Acol 2♠ opening leaves you with no convenient rebid after a 2NT response. Despite the weakness in clubs, opening 2NT is a reasonable compromise. It describes the strength and nature of the hand and if the partnership has the methods to locate a five-card major with opener, 2NT has the fewest flaws.

♠ A Q J 9 5	WEST	NORTH	EAST	SOUTH
♡ A K 6	2NT	No	3♣	No
◇ K Q J	?			
♣ 9 5				

Playing 5-card major Stayman, what do opener's replies to 3♣ mean?

Answer: With a 5-card major, bid it. With no 5-card major, bid 3D (at least one 4-card major) or 3NT (no 4-card major). Many pairs play that after opener's 3◇, responder bids 3♡ to show four spades and 3♠ to show four hearts (puppet Stayman) in order to ensure that opener becomes the declarer if a 4-4 major fit exists.

Here opener bids 3♠ and partner raises that to game.

♠ A Q J 9 5		♠ 10 4 3
♡ A K 6		♡ 7 5 2
◇ K Q J		◇ A 10 7 4
♣ 9 5		♣ 8 3 2

Against 4♠, North starts with the king of clubs, the ace of clubs and a third club which you ruff. How should you continue to give yourself the best chance of making your game?

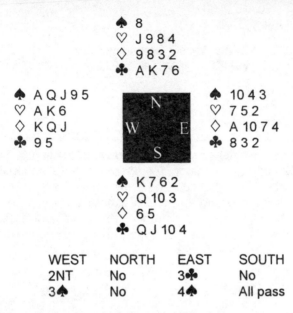

```
                 ♠ 8
                 ♡ J 9 8 4
                 ♦ 9 8 3 2
                 ♣ A K 7 6
♠ A Q J 9 5                        ♠ 10 4 3
♡ A K 6          N                 ♡ 7 5 2
♦ K Q J       W     E              ♦ A 10 7 4
♣ 9 5            S                 ♣ 8 3 2
                 ♠ K 7 6 2
                 ♡ Q 10 3
                 ♦ 6 5
                 ♣ Q J 10 4
```

WEST	NORTH	EAST	SOUTH
2NT	No	3♣	No
3♠	No	4♠	All pass

Declarer must ruff the third club since there may well be a loser in trumps. Having lost only two tricks so far, declarer can afford to lose a trump trick, as the heart loser can be discarded on the fourth diamond later. What then is the problem?

If trumps are 3-2, declarer can misplay the hand and succeed but there is a danger if trumps break 4-1. Suppose at trick 4, declarer plays ace of spades, followed by the queen of spades. South holds off and declarer is doomed. If he tries to run the diamonds, South ruffs the third round and cashes the trump king. If instead West plays a third trump, South wins and plays a fourth club.

Sound technique in such cases often revolves around leaving a trump in dummy to take care of the void suit. The solution here is to lead the queen of spades at trick 4. If South wins, it is all over. If South plays low, continue with the jack of spades. If South ducks this, declarer can avoid a trump loser, while if South takes the spade king now and leads a fourth club, declarer can ruff in dummy, return to hand with a heart and draw South's trumps.

10. You, West, hold:

♠ 8 3   Dealer West : Both vulnerable
♡ A Q 7

WEST	NORTH	EAST	SOUTH
?			

♦ A K J 9 2
♣ 10 8 3

What should West open?

Answer: You have 14 HCP and a balanced hand, counting one extra point for your 5-card suit, treat the hand as 15 points and so too strong to open 1NT. Start with 1♦.

♠ 8 3
♡ A Q 7
♦ A K J 9 2
♣ 10 8 3

WEST	NORTH	EAST	SOUTH
1♦	No	1♠	No
1NT	No	3♣	No
?			

What now?

Answer: Partner has a strong hand with both black suits but with all your strength in the red suits, you should rebid 3NT. This denies three-card support for spades as well.

♠ 8 3
♡ A Q 7
♦ A K J 9 2
♣ 10 8 3

WEST	NORTH	EAST	SOUTH
1♦	No	1♠	No
1NT	No	3♣	No
3NT	No	4♣	No
?			

And now?

Answer: 4♣ shows serious slam prospects and you should cue-bid 4♦ to show club support and diamond control.

♠ 8 3   ♠ A K 7 4 2
♡ A Q 7   ♡ 3
♦ A K J 9 2   ♦ Q 8
♣ 10 8 3   ♣ K Q J 9 2

You finish in 6NT and North leads the ♠Q. How would you play?

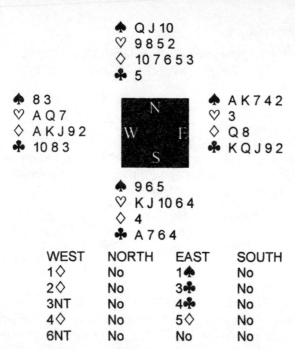

```
                    ♠ Q J 10
                    ♡ 9 8 5 2
                    ◇ 10 7 6 5 3
                    ♣ 5
  ♠ 8 3                                    ♠ A K 7 4 2
  ♡ A Q 7                                  ♡ 3
  ◇ A K J 9 2                              ◇ Q 8
  ♣ 10 8 3                                 ♣ K Q J 9 2
                    ♠ 9 6 5
                    ♡ K J 10 6 4
                    ◇ 4
                    ♣ A 7 6 4
```

WEST	NORTH	EAST	SOUTH
1◇	No	1♠	No
2◇	No	3♣	No
3NT	No	4♣	No
4◇	No	5◇	No
6NT	No	No	No

The actual auction above was based on the Precision system where the 1◇ opening does not promise length in diamonds. 5◇ was not forcing but with a maximum and hearts well held, West unhesitatingly jumped to 6NT.

With two spades, one heart and five almost certain diamond tricks, the instinctive play is to knock out the club ace at trick 2. Suppose you do that and South switches to a heart after taking the ♣A. What would you do? As a favourable diamond break is far more likely than the 50% heart finesse, it would be natural to rise with the heart ace. 6NT would then fail.

Bob Rowlands, West in an English Teams Championship, knew he needed the heart finesse because he tested the diamonds first, a discovery play which could not cost. If they behaved, the clubs could wait. When South showed out on the second diamond, Rowlands switched to clubs. South won and switched to a heart but Rowlands finessed and made the slam. The diamond play is easy enough but it is important to see it at the table and not in the *post mortem*.

11. You, West, hold:

♠ A J 9 8 5 4 2   Dealer North : North-South vulnerable
♡ 9 3
◇ A 6
♣ 8 2

WEST	NORTH	EAST	SOUTH
	1♡	No	3♡
?			

What should West do?

Answer: You have a good, long suit but you do not have a very strong hand. To enter the auction at the three-level one would normally expect better than this. Nevertheless it would be dreadful to pass. The opponents may be able to make game and you may have a very cheap sacrifice, especially at this vulnerability. It is also no great stretch of imagination for your side to be able to make four spades.

Some would jump to 4♠ but this would be misguided. If partner has a singleton spade and one defensive trick, you are likely to defeat 4♡, while 4♠ doubled could be expensive. If you can trust partner, it is quite enough to bid 3♠. If partner has support, partner is likely to raise you to 4♠ anyway and if partner is short in spades, you will defend if they bid further.

Partner is unlikely to be misled about your strength. The opponents have opened and made a limit raise. That will usually be 22 HCP or more their way. The more points partner holds, the more obvious it will be that you have bid on length rather than strength. If partner has some scattered values and 3+ support for spades, you can count on a raise to 4♠.

	♠ A J 9 8 5 4 2		♠ 10 7 3
	♡ 9 3	N	♡ 8 4
	◇ A 6	W E	◇ Q 9
	♣ 8 2	S	♣ A Q 10 7 6 3

Over your 3♠, North passes and East raises to 4♠, passed out. North leads the ♡K. South overtakes with the ♡A and returns the ♡2, won by North who switches to the ◇J. Plan your play.

As North passed 3♠, East might have passed, too. How would you play in 3♠ after the same start?

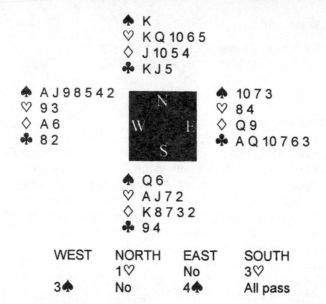

```
              ♠ K
              ♡ K Q 10 6 5
              ◇ J 10 5 4
              ♣ K J 5
♠ A J 9 8 5 4 2              ♠ 10 7 3
♡ 9 3                        ♡ 8 4
◇ A 6                        ◇ Q 9
♣ 8 2                        ♣ A Q 10 7 6 3
              ♠ Q 6
              ♡ A J 7 2
              ◇ K 8 7 3 2
              ♣ 9 4
```

WEST	NORTH	EAST	SOUTH
	1♡	No	3♡
3♠	No	4♣	All pass

With two heart tricks already lost and a certain spade loser, you cannot afford to lose a diamond. Where can you dispose of it? The only hope is on the clubs.

The deal arose in an England Trial. Jeremy Flint, West, was quite certain that South held the ◇K. Otherwise why overtake the ♡K and return a heart? If North held the ◇K, South would have shifted to a diamond at trick 2.

Flint won with the ace of diamonds and, although chances for success were slim, he immediately led a low club, finessing the ten when North played low. A spade to the ace was followed by another club: jack, queen. South ruffed the ace of clubs but Flint discarded the ◇6 and the game was home.

When you need the cards to lie in a certain way for success, assume they do lie that way and play accordingly. Any chance, however remote, is better than no chance at all. Note that you cannot afford to cash the ♠A before finessing the ♣10.

Playing in 3♠, declarer should play low on the ◇J and win with the ◇A. Cash the ♠A and exit with a diamond. South is endplayed upon winning with the ◇K and you thus avoid a club loser, even if South started with the ♣K.

12. You, East, hold:

♠ A K 10 9 8 2	Dealer South : East-West vulnerable			
♡ A K 5 4 3	WEST	NORTH	EAST	SOUTH
◇ A				3◇
♣ A	No	No	?	

What action should East take?

Answer: With only two losers (counting the first three rounds of each suit) you have potential for eleven tricks if a trump fit exists and chances of a fit in one of the majors are excellent. It would be too timid to bid just game with 4♠, say, and anyway hearts may be a better trump suit for the partnership. Best is to bid 4◇, played these days as showing a major two-suiter and not necessarily any better than a five-loser hand (since it is sensible to play partner for two tricks after an enemy pre-empt).

♠ A K 10 9 8 2	WEST	NORTH	EAST	SOUTH
♡ A K 5 4 3				3◇
◇ A	No	No	4◇	No
♣ A	4♠	No	?	

What now?

Answer: As 4◇ has not promised a huge hand, you are worth more. 6♠ would be sensible, especially as partner preferred spades to hearts, but a grand slam is not out of the question. Asking for aces and kings yields no useful information and to cue-bid in either minor implies worry about the other minor. What you need from partner are useful cards in the majors. The best way to suggest a grand slam and focus partner's attention on the majors is with a jump to 6◇.

♠ Q J 7		♠ A K 10 9 8 2
♡ 10 2	N	♡ A K 5 4 3
◇ 7 4 3 2	W E	◇ A
♣ 8 6 5 2	S	♣ A

You have ended in 6♠ and North leads the ◇ 10. Plan the play.

```
              ♠ 6
              ♡ Q J 9 7 6
              ◇ 10
              ♣ K J 10 9 7 4

♠ Q J 7                        ♠ A K 10 9 8 2
♡ 10 2          N              ♡ A K 5 4 3
◇ 7 4 3 2    W     E           ◇ A
♣ 8 6 5 2       S              ♣ A

              ♠ 5 4 3
              ♡ 8
              ◇ K Q J 9 8 6 5
              ♣ Q 3
```

WEST	NORTH	EAST	SOUTH
			3◇
No	No	4◇	No
4♠	No	6◇	No
6♠	No	No	No

On seeing dummy, you regret your timidity in bidding only 6♠. The grand slam in spades is excellent, needing only a 4-2 or 3-3 split in hearts, about an 84% chance. If partner can insist on a small slam, your spade holding coupled with the doubleton in hearts would justify 7♠. After all, you might have had nothing.

It is too late to worry about that. Focus on giving 6♠ your best shot. When everything seems rosy, always ask, 'What could go wrong?' Here the danger is a 5-1 split in hearts, not far-fetched at around a 15% chance. If you start with ♡A and ♡K, South ruffs and returns a trump, leaving you a trick short.

The safety play to cater for hearts 5-1 is to cash a top heart at trick 2 and concede a heart at trick 3. You can then easily ruff dummy's two remaining heart losers in your hand. If North wins and returns a trump, win in dummy, ruff a heart, cross to ♣A and ruff another heart. A club ruff to dummy allows you to draw the missing trumps and claim.

Playing pairs you would forego the safety play. Win ◇A, cash ♡A and ♡K and hope to make all thirteen tricks.

13. You, West, hold:

♠ 5 3   Dealer West : Nil vulnerable
♡ K 6   WEST   NORTH   EAST   SOUTH
◇ Q J 10   ?
♣ A J 10 9 8 2

What would you do as dealer?

Answer: Did we hear you say 'Pass'?! Wash out your mouth with soap and never use that four-letter word again when you hold such a good hand. 11 HCP plus two tens plus a strong 6-card suit would be opened by every strong player. The meek may inherit the earth but they lose at bridge.

♠ 5 3   WEST   NORTH   EAST   SOUTH
♡ K 6   1♣   No   1♡   No
◇ Q J 10   2♣   No   2♠   No
♣ A J 10 9 8 2 ?

What do you understand by 2♠? What do you do now?

Answer: 2♠ is forcing for one round and normally shows 10 points or more. Partner may have four spades but need not have. 2♠ may be merely a spade stopper, trying to focus your attention on the need for a diamond stopper for no-trumps. Responder may have five hearts but this is not guaranteed.

With three hearts, your priority would be to give delayed support for hearts. As you do not have secondary support, the next priority is to bid no-trumps if you have a stopper in the unbid suit. Here you should bid 2NT. To bid 3♣ would imply no stopper in diamonds. If you were a bit stronger, say A-J-10 in diamonds, you would be strong enough to jump to 3NT.

♠ 5 3   ♠ A K 7 6
♡ K 6   N   ♡ J 8 7 5 2
◇ Q J 10   W   E ◇ A 8 2
♣ A J 10 9 8 2   ♣ K
                S

Against 3NT, North leads the ◇4. How will you make nine tricks?

```
                    ♠ J 8
                    ♡ A 9 4
                    ◇ K 9 7 4 3
                    ♣ Q 4 3
   ♠ 5 3                                 ♠ A K 7 6
   ♡ K 6            N                     ♡ J 8 7 5 2
   ◇ Q J 10      W     E                  ◇ A 8 2
   ♣ A J 10 9 8 2    S                    ♣ K
                    ♠ Q 10 9 4 2
                    ♡ Q 10 3
                    ◇ 6 5
                    ♣ 7 6 5
```

WEST	NORTH	EAST	SOUTH
1♣	No	1♡	No
2♣	No	2♠	No
2NT	No	3NT	All pass

As always, start by counting your tricks. If North has the ◇K, you have three tricks there, plus two in spades and five from clubs, assuming you have to concede a trick to the ♣Q. Before playing from dummy, check whether there are any problems.

Here there is one snag. Entries to the West hand are less than abundant. If you play low in dummy and win the first trick in hand, you need South to hold the ♡A so that the ♡K is your entry after the clubs are set up. This is no more than a 50% chance. Why settle for 50% when almost 100% is available?

Even if North's ◇K were visible to West, the diamond finesse should still be rejected. Take the ◇A at trick one and continue with the ♣K, overtaking with your ♣A. Continue with top clubs until the ♣Q is taken. Whatever the defenders play, nothing can prevent declarer returning to hand by leading diamonds twice from dummy and then scoring the remaining club tricks.

On the actual layout, there is no defence to this line. There can be some heart positions which would lay declarer low (if the defence shifts to a heart on winning with the ♣Q) but the recommended line is by far the best chance.

14. You, West, hold:

♠ A K Q 10 9 2   Dealer West : Both vulnerable
♡ A Q 6   WEST   NORTH   EAST   SOUTH
♢ A   ?
♣ Q 9 2

What would you do as dealer?

Answer: Acol Twos and Benjamin Twos can cope but if playing weak twos with 2♣ as the only force, you have to overbid or underbid. The hand is too strong for 1♠ and not enough for a game-force 2♣ opening. In such situations, prefer to overbid and open this one with 2♣. Better to be too high occasionally than not high enough. It would be silly to open 1♠, have it passed out and find partner with the ♡K and three low spades.

♠ A K Q 10 9 2   Dealer West : Both vulnerable
♡ A Q 6   WEST   NORTH   EAST   SOUTH
♢ A   2♣   No   2♢   No
♣ Q 9 2   ?

What next?

Answer: 2♠ is quite enough. While your spades are very strong, you need not insist on spades. If partner were to bid 3♡ next, a heart contract is likely to be best.

Over 2♠, partner bids 3♠, slam-encouraging despite the 2♢ negative, but as you are sub-minimum anyway, you bid just 4♠.

♠ A K Q 10 9 2   ♠ 8 4 3
♡ A Q 6   ♡ 7 5 2
♢ A   ♢ Q J 10 3
♣ Q 9 2   ♣ K 10 6

Against 4♠, North leads the nine of diamonds. Declarer plays the queen, tempting a cover, but South sensibly plays low. Trumps are drawn but it takes three rounds, North discarding two low diamonds. How should declarer continue?

```
                    ♠ 6
                    ♡ J 8 4 3
                    ◇ 9 8 7 4
                    ♣ 8 7 5 3
♠ A K Q 10 9 2                      ♠ 8 4 3
♡ A Q 6                            ♡ 7 5 2
◇ A                                ◇ Q J 10 3
♣ Q 9 2                            ♣ K 10 6
                    ♠ J 7 5
                    ♡ K 10 9
                    ◇ K 6 5 2
                    ♣ A J 4
```

WEST	NORTH	EAST	SOUTH
2♣	No	2◇	No
2♠	No	3♠	No
4♠	No	No	No

The declarer was Mr. G.C.H.Fox, author and former bridge columnist for Britain's *Daily Telegraph* newspaper. He tried the ◇Q on North's ◇9 lead in the hope that South might cover but South correctly played low. It is a losing move to cover an honour when two or more equal honours are visible in dummy and the initial lead marks declarer with the ace.

Declarer then drew trumps and needed to deal with the potential four losers, two in hearts and two in clubs. All would be well if North held the jack of clubs but declarer could also deal with South holding the missing club honours provided that South held the king of hearts as well.

How could declarer manage to force an entry to dummy if South held the ace and jack of clubs? If the queen were led, South would duck if possible. The next club would be taken and a third club cashed. A fourth club or the ◇K exit might leave declarer with two heart losers.

To cater for the clubs lying badly, Fox led the nine of clubs and ran it. Nice move as long as you think of it in time. Even if South held four clubs, he was powerless.

15. You, West, hold:

♠ A	Dealer West : Both vulnerable			
♡ A Q 4	WEST	NORTH	EAST	SOUTH
◇ A K Q J	?			
♣ Q 7 6 5 2				

What would you do as dealer?

Answer: This is a very difficult hand to bid in any standard, natural system. To open 1♣ with 22 HCP risks being passed out when game could be easy (opposite ♡K-x-x-x-x, for example).

It is better to start with 2♣, though later bids may become awkward, while even a 2NT opening would not be overly fanciful.

♠ A	Dealer West : Both vulnerable			
♡ A Q 4	WEST	NORTH	EAST	SOUTH
◇ A K Q J	2♣	2♠	No	No
♣ Q 7 6 5 2	?			

What do you do now?

Answer: Playing takeout doubles here makes double easy. Otherwise, you would have to continue with 3♣.

♠ A	WEST	NORTH	EAST	SOUTH
♡ A Q 4	2♣	2♠	No	No
◇ A K Q J	Double	No	3♣	No
♣ Q 7 6 5 2	?			

What now?

Answer: Slam is not impossible. Bid 4♣ to set the trump suit.

♠ A		♠ 8 6 4 3
♡ A Q 4		♡ 10 9 6
◇ A K Q J		◇ 7 5 3
♣ Q 7 6 5 2		♣ A 8 3

You end in 5♣ and North leads the ♠K. Plan the play.

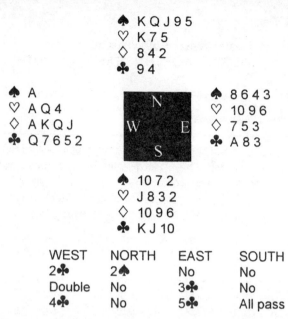

```
                    ♠ K Q J 9 5
                    ♡ K 7 5
                    ◇ 8 4 2
                    ♣ 9 4
   ♠ A                              ♠ 8 6 4 3
   ♡ A Q 4                          ♡ 10 9 6
   ◇ A K Q J          N             ◇ 7 5 3
   ♣ Q 7 6 5 2      W   E           ♣ A 8 3
                      S
                    ♠ 10 7 2
                    ♡ J 8 3 2
                    ◇ 10 9 6
                    ♣ K J 10
```

WEST	NORTH	EAST	SOUTH
2♣	2♠	No	No
Double	No	3♣	No
4♣	No	5♣	All pass

Partner had a tough time after your takeout double and had not the slightest interest in slam after 4♣. Clearly if all you needed for slam was the ♣A, you could have asked for aces. Partner's main relief was that you would have to play the hand.

With at least one loser in hearts and in clubs, you will need some luck here. North is likely to hold at least one king outside spades and your best chance is to play South for the jack of hearts. How can that be accomplished?

The late Jean-Michel Boulenger, a French international, showed how. He led the queen of hearts at trick two. If South held the ♡K, he would later play for North to hold the king of clubs doubleton. As it was, North won and led another spade.

Declarer ruffed and crossed to the ace of clubs. He then led the ♡10 and let it run when South played low. It would not have helped South to cover as the ♡9 would have given declarer access to dummy.

Having eliminated a heart loser *and remaining in dummy*, declarer now led a second round of trumps to his queen. He thus lost just one heart and one club. Bien joué.

16. You, West, hold:

♠ K J 4   Dealer West : East-West vulnerable
♡ K 8 5
◇ A 8 7 5 4
♣ A 7

WEST	NORTH	EAST	SOUTH
?			

What is your plan of bidding?

Answer: Playing a strong no-trump, you would open 1NT. Playing a 12-14 1NT, you open 1◇ and rebid in no-trumps.

♠ K J 4   Dealer West : East-West vulnerable
♡ K 8 5
◇ A 8 7 5 4
♣ A 7

WEST	NORTH	EAST	SOUTH
1◇	No	2♣	No
?			

What do you do now?

Answer: 2NT shows 15+ points balanced and is forcing after the two-over-one response. Even if partner bid 3♣ next, showing a weak hand with long clubs, you would bid 3NT.

♠ K J 4
♡ K 8 5
◇ A 8 7 5 4
♣ A 7

WEST	NORTH	EAST	SOUTH
1◇	No	2♣	No
2NT	No	3◇	No
?			

What next?

Answer: Partner is either concerned about one of the majors or has slam interest. In either case, you should bid 3NT since both majors are stopped and you are absolutely minimum.

♠ K J 4   ♠ 10 6
♡ K 8 5   ♡ 7 4
◇ A 8 7 5 4   ◇ K J 3
♣ A 7   ♣ K Q 10 9 6 3

North leads the queen of hearts against 3NT. Plan your play.

```
                    ♠ 9 7 5 2
                    ♡ A Q J 9 2
                    ◇ Q 6 2
                    ♣ 4
♠ K J 4                             ♠ 10 6
♡ K 8 5         N                   ♡ 7 4
◇ A 8 7 5 4   W     E               ◇ K J 3
♣ A 7           S                   ♣ K Q 10 9 6 3
                    ♠ A Q 8 3
                    ♡ 10 6 3
                    ◇ 10 9
                    ♣ J 8 5 2
```

WEST	NORTH	EAST	SOUTH
1◇	No	2♣	No
2NT	No	3◇	No
3NT	No	No	No

It is vital to take the ♡K at trick one. Otherwise a spade switch to South's ace and a heart return gives the defence six tricks.

Counting tricks, you can see that if the clubs break favourably you have nine tricks. Before tackling the clubs, ask yourself 'What if the clubs do not break?'

Declarer cannot afford to give up a club as the opponents can cash enough tricks to set the contract. So, if the clubs play for only three tricks, declarer will need five tricks from diamonds.

The best chance for five diamond tricks is to finesse North for the queen. It would be unwise to play on diamonds first since if the diamond finesse fails, you could go down in 3NT with the clubs breaking all along.

To combine your chances in the minors, tackle the clubs first but in such a way that does not jeopardise your best play in diamonds. The solution is to play the ♣7 to dummy's king at trick two, followed by a club back to the ace. If the clubs run, it is all over. When the clubs are found wanting, you have the lead in your hand for a low diamond to dummy's jack, followed by the ◇K, ♣Q cashed and the ◇3 back to your ace. Bingo!

17. You, East, hold:

♠ A 6 5 4   Dealer West : East-West vulnerable
♡ K 6 4   WEST   NORTH   EAST   SOUTH
◊ - - -   1♡   2♠ (1)   ?
♣ A Q J 9 3 2   (1) Intermediate, 11-15 HCP and a 6+ suit

What should East do?

Answer: Playing for penalties is not attractive when you have length in partner's suit. With game almost certain and slam possible, you should make the natural bid, 3♣.

♠ A 6 5 4   WEST   NORTH   EAST   SOUTH
♡ K 6 4   1♡   2♠   3♣   No
◊ - - -   3◊   No   ?
♣ A Q J 9 3 2

What can you deduce from partner's rebid?

Answer: With two four-card suits, it is normal practice to open in the cheaper suit. One of the benefits of that approach is that when opener rebids in a lower-ranking suit, you can deduce that opener has at least five cards in the first bid suit. Opener may breach this approach with a 4-4 pattern if holding stoppers in each short suit and intending to rebid in no-trumps.

What do you do now?

Answer: It is best to support hearts, but how many? You are too strong to settle just for game. To jump to 5♡ in this auction would seek spade control rather than strong trumps and so you should bite the bullet and jump to slam.

♠ 7   ♠ A 6 5 4
♡ A Q 7 5 3   ♡ K 6 4
◊ K 5 4 2   ◊ - - -
♣ K 10 5   ♣ A Q J 9 3 2

North leads the king of spades against 6♡. Plan the play.

```
                  ♠ K Q J 10 9 3
                  ♡ 8
                  ◇ A J 10
                  ♣ 8 6 4
  ♠ 7                                    ♠ A 6 5 4
  ♡ A Q 7 5 3        N                   ♡ K 6 4
  ◇ K 5 4 2      W       E               ◇ - - -
  ♣ K 10 5           S                   ♣ A Q J 9 3 2
                  ♠ 8 2
                  ♡ J 10 9 2
                  ◇ Q 9 8 7 6 3
                  ♣ 7
```

WEST	NORTH	EAST	SOUTH
1♡	2♠	3♣	No
3◇	No	6♡	All pass

On seeing dummy you regret not supporting partner's clubs, for 6♣ seems a breeze. It's no use crying over spilt milk and as long as you make 6♡, there will be no acrimony in the *post mortem* (not that there should ever be any acrimony in your games).

Counting your tricks, you can see six clubs, one spade and five hearts if they split 3-2. With twelve tricks easy on a normal trump break, you naturally see whether you can cope with a 4-1 break. With only four heart winners you need a trick elsewhere and that can come from a diamond ruff in dummy.

At the table declarer erred by drawing two rounds of trumps at tricks two and three. When the bad break was revealed, he switched to clubs but South did not ruff in until the third round. Now declarer slid to an ignominious three-trick defeat.

After taking the ♠A, to cater for a possible 4-1 break in hearts (a touch more than a 1-in-4 chance), the best move is to duck a round of trumps. You ruff the likely spade continuation, ruff a diamond in dummy and cash the ♡K. If hearts are 3-2, ruff another spade and draw the last trump.

When trumps turn out to be 4-1, play a club to your king, draw the remaining trumps and then run the clubs.

18. You, West, hold:

♠ J 9 3   Dealer West : East-West vulnerable
♡ A 10 2   WEST   NORTH   EAST   SOUTH
♢ A K Q 5 4 ?
♣ 6 5

What action would you take as dealer?

Answer: Playing a 12-14 1NT, you should open this hand 1♢.
You have 14 HCP and a balanced hand but you should
upgrade the hand by one point for the five-card suit. That
brings you to 15 points, too good for 1NT, and the ♡10 is
another positive feature.

♠ J 9 3   Dealer West : East-West vulnerable
♡ A 10 2   WEST   NORTH   EAST   SOUTH
♢ A K Q 5 4 1♢   No   3♢   No
♣ 6 5   ?

What do you do after partner's limit raise?

Answer: With 14 HCP, you should accept partner's invitation to
game but do not push on to 5♢. You would like to bid 3NT but
what about the weakness in both black suits, especially clubs?

Life and bridge offer no guarantees and so take a chance. It
is best to grasp the nettle and bid 3NT. Even if you bid 3♡,
partner would not know which black suit posed the problem. As
partner has so little in diamonds, partner's high cards may well
be in the black suits. In addition, there might be nine tricks on
top even if one of the black suits is unguarded. For example,
give East something like ♠ x x x ♡ K x x ♢ J x x x ♣ A K x and
3NT is highly likely to succeed. You cannot expect guarantees.

♠ J 9 3   ♠ A 8
♡ A 10 2   ♡ 7 4 3
♢ A K Q 5 4   ♢ 10 9 6 2
♣ 6 5   ♣ A Q 9 2

North leads the six of hearts against 3NT. Plan your play.

```
                    ♠ Q 7 5 2
                    ♡ K J 9 6 5
                    ◇ - - -
                    ♣ J 10 4 3
♠ J 9 3                                    ♠ A 8
♡ A 10 2          N                        ♡ 7 4 3
◇ A K Q 5 4    W     E                      ◇ 10 9 6 2
♣ 6 5              S                        ♣ A Q 9 2
                    ♠ K 10 6 4
                    ♡ Q 8
                    ◇ J 8 7 3
                    ♣ K 8 7
```

WEST	NORTH	EAST	SOUTH
1◇	No	3◇	No
3NT	No	No	No

3NT is pretty good, no worse than the 50% club finesse if you have five diamond tricks. Your first move should be to duck the first heart. As the three lowest hearts are visible, North's ♡6 could be from four or from five. To take the first heart would reduce your chances of success if hearts are 5-2. It is true that a spade switch might be damaging but such a switch is unlikely and anyway, it would leave you no worse off than if you had won the first heart.

When South continues with a second heart, you should take the ace. If hearts were 5-2, South has no more hearts and if hearts were 4-3, you can lose no more than three heart tricks.

Next you should cash the ace of diamonds to check that they do break. When North shows out, you know that you will need to run the ten through South later. Also, take care to play the ◇6 from dummy, otherwise the diamond suit might be blocked later.

Your next move is to lead a club and finesse dummy's nine, not the queen first. The chance of North holding both the jack and ten of clubs is only 25% but it costs you nothing to try. When the ♣9 forces out South's king, you are home. Had the ♣9 lost to the ten or jack, you would have finessed the ♣Q next time. Note that it is of no avail for North to split the club honours.

19. You, East, hold:

♠ 9 8 4 2
♥ Q 6
♦ 10 7 4 3
♣ K 8 4

Dealer West : Nil vulnerable

WEST	NORTH	EAST	SOUTH
2NT (1)	No	?	
(1) 20-22			

What action should East take?

Answer: Clearly you will push on to game (even four points would be enough to have a go), but you should explore the possibility of 4♠. Partner might have four spades and so you should bid 3♣, Stayman, to ask about opener's majors.

If opener rebids 3♦, no major, you will rebid 3NT.

What if opener's reply to 3♣ is 3♥?

Answer: Opener might be 4-4 in the majors and if so, would bid 3♥ in reply to 3♣. You should rebid 3NT anyway. Since you were interested in a major and have rejected hearts, clearly you must hold four spades. If 4-4 in the majors, opener will then rebid 4♠. The advantage here is that opener will be the declarer whether the contract is 3NT, 4♥ or 4♠.

What if 2NT might include a 5-card major?

Answer: If this is permitted (and it is sensible to do so), it is advisable to play 3♣ as 5-card major Stayman. 3♣ then asks, 'Do you have a 5-card major?' Opener bids 3♥ or 3♠ with five, 3♦ with no 5-card major but at least one 4-card major and 3NT with no 4+ major. Here if opener bids 3♦ in reply to 3♣, East should rebid 3♥, puppet Stayman, to show four spades, again so that opener would be the declarer if a 4-4 spade fit exists.

♠ A 7 3
♥ A 7
♦ A K 6
♣ A J 10 9 2

♠ 9 8 4 2
♥ Q 6
♦ 10 7 4 3
♣ K 8 4

In reply to 3♣, 5-card major Stayman, West rebid 3NT and North led the ♥J, covered by the queen, king, and ace. Plan the play.

45

```
                    ♠ J 10 6
                    ♡ J 10 9 5 4 2
                    ◇ Q 8 5
                    ♣ 5
♠ A 7 3                                      ♠ 9 8 4 2
♡ A 7                                        ♡ Q 6
◇ A K 6              N                        ◇ 10 7 4 3
♣ A J 10 9 2      W     E                    ♣ K 8 4
                     S
                    ♠ K Q 5
                    ♡ K 8 3
                    ◇ J 9 2
                    ♣ Q 7 6 3
```

To make 3NT you need five club tricks. With eight cards missing the queen, finessing is clearly superior to playing off the ace and king in the hope that the club queen will drop. Here you can play either opponent for the ♣Q and if clubs are 3-2, it would be a simple 50% proposition which way to finesse. However, the 4-1 break occurs so often (c. 28% of the time) that you must take it into account. To guard against a singleton queen, you should play off a top honour first but if you cash the ♣A you can no longer catch ♣Q-x-x-x in the North hand. However, if you run the ♣J for a first-round finesse to cater for four clubs with North, you risk losing to ♣Q singleton with South.

That makes it best to play South for the ♣Q (also because North is likely to have greater heart length than South and therefore likely to be shorter in clubs). You can cash the ♣K to cater for a singleton queen and continue with a club finesse against South.

An important precaution is necessary. If you lead the ♣2 to the king and finesse on the way back, the lead will be in the West hand with no entry to dummy to repeat the finesse. You should therefore start by leading the ♣J. Prefer the jack to the nine or ten since an unwary North might cover the jack with the queen.

When North plays low, rise with dummy's king and continue with the eight of clubs. If South plays low, let the eight run. When it wins you are still in dummy to repeat the finesse.

20. You, West, hold:

♠ A Q 2	Dealer North : Both vulnerable			
♡ K 5	WEST	NORTH	EAST	SOUTH
◇ Q J 8 2		1♠	No	No
♣ A Q 7 3	?			

What action should West take?

Answer: After an opponent opens, bidding in the pass-out seat is quite different from bidding in the direct seat. You need clear agreements how to show the ranges for your balanced hands in the pass-out seat. Quite a sensible treatment is to play 1NT as 11-16 (using a 2♣ reply as a range finder: opener bids 2◇ with 11-12, 2♡, 2♠ or 2NT with 13-14 and at the three-level with 15-16), 2NT as 17-18 balanced and to double with 19+ balanced. There is more value in 2NT as a natural re-opening bid than to show both minors since there is no need here to suggest a sacrifice in 5♣ or 5◇ to partner.

On that basis West would bid 2NT and subsequent bidding follows the same path as after a 2NT opening.

♠ A Q 2	WEST	NORTH	EAST	SOUTH
♡ K 5		1♠	No	No
◇ Q J 8 2	2NT	No	3◇*	No
♣ A Q 7 3	?		*Transfer to hearts	

What action should West take?

Answer: If you play transfers over a 2NT opening, you should play them in this auction as well. Therefore West should bid 3♡ as responder may be very weak with long hearts. You are not permitted to reject the transfer.

♠ A Q 2		♠ 8 5
♡ K 5	N	♡ Q J 7 4 2
◇ Q J 8 2	W E	◇ K 10 5 3
♣ A Q 7 3	S	♣ K 4

Against 3NT, North leads the ♠J, won by the ♠Q. Plan the play.

♠ K J 10 9 4 3
♡ A 6
◇ A 7
♣ 6 5 2

♠ A Q 2      ♠ 8 5
♡ K 5   ♡ Q J 7 4 2
◇ Q J 8 2   ◇ K 10 5 3
♣ A Q 7 3   ♣ K 4

♠ 7 6
♡ 10 9 8 3
◇ 9 6 4
♣ J 10 9 8

WEST	NORTH	EAST	SOUTH
	1♠	No	No
2NT	No	3◇	No
3♡	No	3NT	All pass

With five winners in the blacks, you need four winners from the red suits. If you play the ♡K at trick 2 to knock out the ace, you succeed if hearts are 3-3, but with six cards missing, the 4-2 split occurs more often than the 3-3. On the actual layout, North takes the ace and leads another spade. When the hearts are indeed 4-2 and you shift to diamonds, North takes the ace and cashes spades. If you tackle diamonds first, North can take the ace at once and continue spades. When you lead a heart later, North grabs the ace and cashes spades.

At trick 2, lead the ♡5 from hand, not the ♡K. With the ♡A marked with North, success is certain (unless hearts are 5-1 or 6-0) whether North began with A-x, A-x-x or A-x-x-x in hearts. If North rises with the ace, you have your four tricks in hearts. North plays a second spade to your ace. You unblock the ♡K, cross to the ♣K and run the hearts.

If Norths plays low on the ♡5, dummy's honour wins. With one heart trick in, abandon hearts and shift to diamonds, setting up three tricks there while you still have the spades stopped.

21. You, West, hold:

♠ A K Q J	Dealer West : North-South vulnerable			
♡ K 8 3	WEST	NORTH	EAST	SOUTH
◇ J 6 2	1♠	2◇	Double	No
♣ K Q 6	?			

What do you understand by East's double?

Answer: The rule used to be that a double after partner had bid was for penalties. In that case you would pass and expect to collect heaps. The modern style is to play doubles of suit bids at the one- or two-level as takeout doubles, almost regardless of the preceding auction. For responder's takeout double here, you can expect East to have 4+ hearts and 6+ points.

What do you do, given that East's double is for takeout?

Answer: With 19 points opposite the expected six or more, you should insist on game even though your ◇J may be worthless. As you have no inkling which game to play, bid 3◇. Bidding the enemy suit before suit agreement has been reached indicates the values for game without a clear idea which game is best.

Over 3◇ partner may be able to bid 3♡ to show a five-card suit (you would raise to 4♡) or 3NT if holding a diamond stopper.

♠ A K Q J	WEST	NORTH	EAST	SOUTH
♡ K 8 3	1♠	2◇	Double	No
◇ J 6 2	3◇	No	4♠	No
♣ K Q 6	?			

What now?

Answer: As 3◇ showed your values, there is no reason to bid on.

♠ A K Q J		♠ 9 8 4 3 2
♡ K 8 3	N	♡ A J 4 2
◇ J 6 2	W E	◇ 8 5
♣ K Q 6	S	♣ A J

North leads the ◇Q, followed by the ◇A and then the ◇K. What should you do?

```
                    ♠ 7
                    ♡ 7 6
                    ◇ A K Q 10 7 4
                    ♣ 9 8 4 3

  ♠ A K Q J                              ♠ 9 8 4 3 2
  ♡ K 8 3                                ♡ A J 4 2
  ◇ J 6 2                                ◇ 8 5
  ♣ K Q 6                                ♣ A J

                    ♠ 10 6 5
                    ♡ Q 10 9 5
                    ◇ 9 3
                    ♣ 10 7 5 2
```

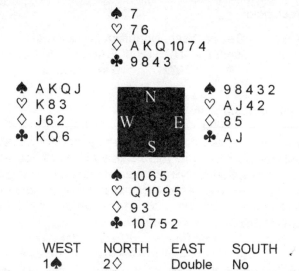

WEST	NORTH	EAST	SOUTH
1♠	2◇	Double	No
3◇	No	4♠	All pass

Double was a curious choice by East but partners have been known to do even stranger things. With eight losers, a limit raise to 3♠ would have been enough. Even if a heart fit happened to exist, it could not be superior to the spade fit.

Some play that after a suit opening and a suit overcall, a bid of the enemy suit by responder shows a limit raise or better. On that basis, 3♠ would be a weaker raise and East would be worth 3◇ here.

Playing in 4♠, you have two losers in diamonds and one in hearts if the ♡Q is offside. What then is the problem?

The third round of diamonds is a potential loser. It may seem that the best hope is to ruff high in dummy but if South can over-ruff and also has the ♡Q, 4♠ will fail.

There is no need to take this risk. Even if North had not overcalled and even if South did not signal 9-then-3 in diamonds, declarer should play the same way. On the third diamond, discard dummy's two of hearts. Declarer wins any switch, draws trumps and discards dummy's other heart loser on the third round of clubs. If North plays a fourth diamond, you ruff in dummy and over-ruff South if necessary.

22. You, West, hold:

♠ A Q J 10 5   Dealer West : Nil vulnerable
♡ Q 8 4   WEST   NORTH   EAST   SOUTH
◇ Q   1♠   No   2♣   No
♣ K Q 8 5   ?

What should West rebid?

Answer: Clearly you should support partner, but how many clubs should you bid? With 16 HCP and a singleton, you are too strong for 3♣, notwithstanding the singleton ◇Q.

Do not jump to game in a minor unless it is clear that there are no slam prospects. To bid 5♣ robs partner of the chance to ask for aces. As East is unlimited, slam is certainly possible.

In standard style, you are worth 4♣. The jump-raise of a minor is forcing to game after a two-over-one response.

In a modern partnership, West might choose a 3◇ 'splinter' rebid. A splinter shows a strong hand with 4+ support for partner and a singleton or void in the suit bid. One advantage of 3◇ is that 3NT is still available if partner is strong in diamonds.

♠ A Q J 10 5   WEST   NORTH   EAST   SOUTH
♡ Q 8 4   1♠   No   2♣   No
◇ Q   4♣   No   4♠   No
♣ K Q 8 5   ?

What should West do now?

Answer: Responder's return to opener's major at game-level is a sign-off. It implies a limit raise with only three trumps. With slam interest, responder should cue-bid or ask with 4NT.

♠ A Q J 10 5   ♠ 6 3 2
♡ Q 8 4   N   ♡ J 2
◇ Q   W   E   ◇ A 5 4 2
♣ K Q 8 5   S   ♣ A J 10 7

Against 4♠, North leads the four of spades. South plays the eight and West wins. How should declarer proceed?

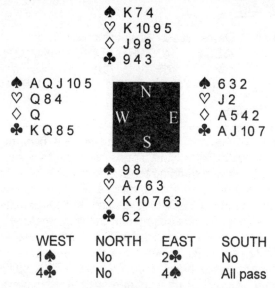

♠ K 7 4
♡ K 10 9 5
◇ J 9 8
♣ 9 4 3

♠ A Q J 10 5
♡ Q 8 4
◇ Q
♣ K Q 8 5

♠ 6 3 2
♡ J 2
◇ A 5 4 2
♣ A J 10 7

♠ 9 8
♡ A 7 6 3
◇ K 10 7 6 3
♣ 6 2

WEST	NORTH	EAST	SOUTH
1♠	No	2♣	No
4♣	No	4♠	All pass

You have a possible spade loser and two heart losers. If you can ruff the third heart, all will be well but there is a problem. If you lead a heart to the jack and South wins, a trump return could lay you low. If you finesse, North might win with the ♠K and play a third trump, eliminating dummy's ruffing power. You will then probably lose one spade and three hearts.

If North does have the ♠K, rising with the ♠A may not help you when South returns a trump. If North can win the next round of hearts and cash the ♠K, you have fared no better.

Your best chance is to cross to dummy with the ◇Q to dummy's ace and then lead dummy's two of hearts. If South has A-K in hearts, this will set up a heart winner for you. On the actual layout, if South rises with the ace to lead a trump, it will no longer matter. As you have not lost an honour to the ♡A, you will be able to set up a heart trick later.

If South plays low on the ♡2, your ♡Q will be taken by North who cannot lead a second trump without losing his trump trick. On any other return, declarer can win and lead a second heart. If South wins this and plays a trump, declarer rises with the ace and ruffs the third heart in dummy.

23. You, West, hold:

♠ Q J 10 6 Dealer West : East-West vulnerable
♥ K J 10 9 5 2

	WEST	NORTH	EAST	SOUTH
♦ A Q 8	1♥	2♣	No	No
♣ - - -	?			

What should West do now?

Answer: When you have a weak opening and an overcall on your left is passed back to you, partner is often angling for penalties if you are short in the overcall suit. If playing negative doubles, partner is unable to double for penalties. Partner is hoping for a balancing double, which will be left in for penalties.

Your hand is suitable for a re-opening double but with a void in their suit, low-level penalties lack appeal, as you are unable to lead trumps for partner. Also, partner is likely to be short in your suit. If your hearts were headed by the A-K, you might still double but with no quick winner in hearts and only one sure entry outside, you are likely to be better off bidding 2♥.

	WEST	NORTH	EAST	SOUTH
♠ Q J 10 6				
♥ K J 10 9 5 2	1♥	2♣	No	No
♦ A Q 8	2♥	No	3♥	No
♣ - - -	?			

Do you accept the invitation or pass?

Answer: You have not promised a strong hand but with your excellent shape, you should push on to 4♥. You have only five losers and so two useful cards with partner should be enough to reduce your losers to three.

♠ Q J 10 6		♠ K 4 2
♥ K J 10 9 5 2	N	♥ A 8 3
♦ A Q 8	W E	♦ 5 4 2
♣ - - -	S	♣ K J 10 2

Against 4♥, North leads the ♠9, low from dummy, and South signals encouragement with the ♠7. How would you continue?

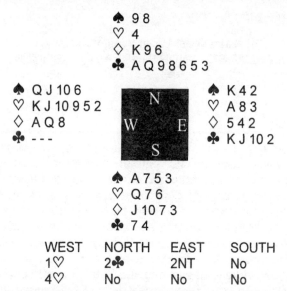

```
              ♠ 9 8
              ♡ 4
              ◇ K 9 6
              ♣ A Q 9 8 6 5 3
♠ Q J 10 6                        ♠ K 4 2
♡ K J 10 9 5 2        N          ♡ A 8 3
◇ A Q 8           W       E      ◇ 5 4 2
♣ - - -                          ♣ K J 10 2
                      S
              ♠ A 7 5 3
              ♡ Q 7 6
              ◇ J 10 7 3
              ♣ 7 4
```

WEST	NORTH	EAST	SOUTH
1♡	2♣	2NT	No
4♡	No	No	No

This auction is better. Avoid playing for penalties when holding three-card support for opener. 2♣ doubled can be defeated by two tricks but that is poor compensation for a vulnerable game.

In 4♡ West has four possible losers, one in each major and two in diamonds if the ◇K is offside (very likely on the bidding).

You wish to ruff a diamond in dummy after discarding a diamond on your fourth spade, but there is a snag. To play off two top hearts will work if hearts are 2-2 but if either player holds ♡Q-x-x, a third trump before you can ruff a diamond will thwart you. If you finesse either way, ♡Q-x-x offside may beat you.

On the reasonable assumption that North has two or three rag spades and the ◇K, the solution is to cash the ♡K, then revert to spades. If South wins and gives North a spade ruff, you draw the last trump and discard a diamond on your fourth spade.

If South takes the ♠A and shifts to a diamond, play the ◇A. Continue with a third spade. If North ruffs, you are safe. If all follow, play the fourth spade. If North ruffs with the ♡Q, dummy over-ruffs. If North ruffs low, discard a diamond from dummy. You can draw the ♡Q later and ruff a diamond in dummy.

If South ruffs the fourth spade, you are safe. If nobody ruffs the fourth spade, you play to ruff a diamond in dummy.

24. You, East, hold:

♠ A 3 2   Dealer West : Both vulnerable
♡ A J 10 6 3   WEST   NORTH   EAST   SOUTH
♢ J 10   1♢   No   1♡   No
♣ 9 4 2   1♠   No   ?

What should East do now?

Answer: It would be a serious error to bid 2♡, which would show extra length in hearts but not extra strength. East is strong enough to invite a game but any natural invitation is flawed. To jump to 3♡ would imply a six-card suit, to raise the spades requires four-card support and a jump to 2NT should include at least one stopper in the unbid suit, clubs.

The solution to such a problem is to bid the fourth-suit, 2♣ here. This is an artificial bid, indicating game interest and seeking further information from opener. Even if East held a stopper in clubs, 2♣ would be advisable to allow opener to show three-card heart support. A 5-3 fit in hearts suggests that 4♡ is likely to fare better than 3NT.

Suppose you have bid 2♣.
What would you do if opener rebid 2NT?

Answer: In standard style, fourth-suit forcing at the one- or two-level is forcing for only one round and a minimum bid in no-trumps or any bid suit is droppable. With a good hand, opener needs to jump to insist on game. Opener's 2NT implies a minimum opening and responder should pass. Opener should be 4-2-5-2 or 4-1-5-3 because of the failure to open 1NT.

If opener rebids 2♡, make a further try with 3♡ since if opener has a minimum with three hearts, the shape figures to be 4-3-5-1.

♠ Q J 5 4   ♠ A 3 2
♡ 7   ♡ A J 10 6 3
♢ A K Q 9 2   ♢ J 10
♣ K J 5   ♣ 9 4 2

Against 3NT, North leads ♣7, South playing ♣Q. Plan the play.

```
            ♠ 10 7
            ♡ K 9 2
            ◇ 8 7 5
            ♣ A 10 8 7 3
♠ Q J 5 4              ♠ A 3 2
♡ 7            N       ♡ A J 10 6 3
◇ A K Q 9 2  W   E     ◇ J 10
♣ K J 5        S       ♣ 9 4 2
            ♠ K 9 8 6
            ♡ Q 8 5 4
            ◇ 6 4 3
            ♣ Q 6
```

WEST	NORTH	EAST	SOUTH
1◇	No	1♡	No
1♠	No	2♣	No
3NT	No	No	No

You started with seven tricks on top and the lead has given you an eighth. The ninth can come from the spades. You can lead the ♠Q and even if this loses to South, your ♠J is now a winner. This will not be of much use if the opponents can take five tricks before you can set up the extra spade trick. On the actual layout, if you capture South's ♣Q and run the ♠Q, South wins and a club return gives North four tricks. One down.

Does that mean that you must resort to prayer, fervently wishing for clubs to be 6-1 or 4-3 or for North to hold the king of spades? Prayers might help but are unnecessary here if declarer tackles the hand correctly.

If West held A-x-x in clubs, a hold-up play at trick one would be automatic. Here one tends to grab the ♣Q instinctively but a hold-up is available without costing you a trick in clubs. Play the ♣5 at trick one. If South switches to another suit, declarer has no problems. If clubs are continued, declarer scores a trick in clubs and when West later runs the ♠Q, South wins but has no club to return to North. If South had a third club, the clubs would be 4-3 and West loses only one spade and three clubs.

25. You, West, hold:

♠ K J 10 2   Dealer West : Both vulnerable
♡ A K Q J 3

WEST	NORTH	EAST	SOUTH
1♡	No	2♡	No
?			

♦ 7
♣ 7 5 4

Do you pass or bid on?

Answer: With 14 HCP and a 5-3-3-2 pattern you would pass but with a singleton, you are worth a further move. You have six losers (two in spades, one diamond and three clubs) which justifies a game invitation. A minimum opening hand usually has seven losers and you are one playing trick stronger.

What bid do you make?

Answer: A simple raise to 3♡ will lead to 4♡ if opener is maximum but you can do better than this. The greatest risk lies in clubs. If partner has strong clubs (or a singleton club), game should be a strong chance but if partner's clubs are weak, game can be hopeless even opposite a maximum raise.

Contrast these two hands:

(a) ♠ Q x x   ♡ x x x x   ♦ K Q J   ♣ J x x

(b) ♠ Q x x   ♡ x x x x   ♦ J x x   ♣ K Q J

Opposite (a), 4♡ is awful but opposite (b), 4♡ is almost a sure thing. To focus partner's attention, bid 3♣, a trial bid which asks partner to bid game in hearts with just one club loser (or two losers and a maximum) but to sign off in 3♡ with three losers in clubs. A singleton club or strength in clubs is what declarer needs.

♠ K J 10 2		♠ 9 5 3
♡ A K Q J 3		♡ 7 5 4 2
♦ 7		♦ A 8 3
♣ 7 5 4		♣ A J 10

Against 4♡, North leads the ♦J. How should declarer play?

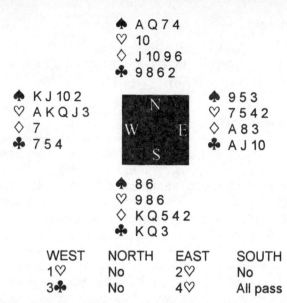

```
              ♠ A Q 7 4
              ♡ 10
              ◇ J 10 9 6
              ♣ 9 8 6 2

♠ K J 10 2                        ♠ 9 5 3
♡ A K Q J 3         N            ♡ 7 5 4 2
◇ 7             W       E        ◇ A 8 3
♣ 7 5 4            S             ♣ A J 10

              ♠ 8 6
              ♡ 9 8 6
              ◇ K Q 5 4 2
              ♣ K Q 3
```

WEST	NORTH	EAST	SOUTH
1♡	No	2♡	No
3♣	No	4♡	All pass

If the ♠Q is onside or North holds an honour in clubs, 4♡ will make. Therefore assume all four cards lie badly and see whether you can deal with that. In time, it will be possible to set up an extra spade trick in hand on which you can discard a club loser from dummy. You can later ruff the third round of clubs in dummy and so lose just two spades and one club.

You cannot afford to tackle spades at once since that would run the risk of a spade ruff. The play is straightforward as long as you do not become mesmerised with the need for a spade finesse. Draw trumps in three rounds and then lead a spade from hand. It does not matter which spade you lead. A tiny benefit in favour of the king of spades is the possibility of a singleton queen of spades.

North can win the spade and shift to a club. You play low from dummy and South wins. With no entry to North for a second club lead without setting up declarer's spades, there is no defence. On a diamond return, declarer ruffs and continues spades. Had North led a club initially, a sensible idea when declarer has indicated weakness there because of the trial bid, 4♡ can be defeated.

26. You, West, hold:

♠ K 7 4	Dealer East : Nil vulnerable		
♡ A 10	WEST	NORTH	EAST	SOUTH
◇ 6 5 2			1♡	1♠
♣ K Q J 6 3	?			

What should West do?

Answer: Some charge at no-trumps like a bull at a gate but the bidding is not a race to see who can bid no-trumps first. This hand might belong in clubs or hearts, perhaps in slam, and if no-trumps is correct, you will reach it later. Make the natural bid of 2♣.

♠ K 7 4	WEST	NORTH	EAST	SOUTH
♡ A 10			1♡	1♠
◇ 6 5 2	2♣	No	2♡	No
♣ K Q J 6 3	?			

And now what?

Answer: Slam is no longer in contention after partner's minimum rebid. No-trumps appeals more now than it did before but it is still too soon to commit to that. If partner has nothing in spades, 4♡ might be the best spot. In addition, no-trumps might play better from partner's side (if partner has Q-x or A-J or Q-10 or similar in spades). Bidding 2♠, the enemy suit, will fetch more information from partner and you will then be better placed to make a decision about the best contract.

♠ K 7 4		♠ Q 10 2
♡ A 10	N	♡ Q J 9 6 3
◇ 6 5 2	W E	◇ A K 10
♣ K Q J 6 3	S	♣ 10 4

Had West in fact bid 2♠, East would have bid 2NT and the best spot of 3NT by East would have been reached. In practice, West rebid a hasty 3NT over 2♡ and your task is to salvage this contract after North leads the ♠6. Plan the play.

```
              ♠ 6 5
              ♡ K 8 7 5
              ◇ 9 8 4 3
              ♣ 9 8 7
♠ K 7 4                          ♠ Q 10 2
♡ A 10          N                ♡ Q J 9 6 3
◇ 6 5 2      W     E             ◇ A K 10
♣ K Q J 6 3     S                ♣ 10 4
              ♠ A J 9 8 3
              ♡ 4 2
              ◇ Q J 7
              ♣ A 5 2
```

The first task is to picture the spade layout. South's overcall
should be based on a decent five-card or longer suit. As you can
see three spade honours, South should hold the other two,
giving South A-J-x-x-x or A-J-x-x-x-x in spades.

Next count your winners. You have three on top and can
easily set up extra tricks in clubs and hearts. In clubs this
entails losing the lead and likewise in hearts if North has the
king. There are tricks galore, but the danger is that the defence
comes to five tricks before you can set up the tricks needed.

Suppose you make the instinctive play of a low spade from
dummy. South plays the ♠8 and you win. You knock out the
♣A and South switches to a heart. With only eight tricks at this
point, you are committed to the heart finesse. North wins and
reverts to spades. Two down. The same ensues if you insert
dummy's ten at trick one, South playing the jack.

If you have visualized the spade position at the outset, the
solution is not too hard. Play the ♠Q from dummy at trick one.
South must win, else you score two spade tricks. South cannot
lead a second spade for you would duck this to the ten and
again make two spade tricks. If South shifts to a heart, you rise
with the ace and knock out the ♣A. As long as North does not
have the ♣A, you are home. When South takes the ♣A, no
return gives you any difficulty.

27. You, West, hold:

♠ A Q 10 6 3   Dealer West : East-West vulnerable
♡ K 7 2   WEST   NORTH   EAST   SOUTH
◇ Q 10 7 4   ?
♣ 6

What should West do as dealer?

Answer: As indicated in Problem #7, as long as you have no wasted points in your singleton, it is worth opening a hand which measures 12 total points, counting HCP and adding one point for each card beyond four cards in a suit. This hand measures 12 such points and, an important consideration, you have no rebid problems. Open 1♠.

What do you rebid over (a) 1NT? (b) 2♣? (c) 2◇? (d) 2♡?

Answer: Over 1NT or 2♣, show your second suit (2◇) and over 2◇ or 2♡, support partner's suit.

♠ A Q 10 6 3   Dealer West : East-West vulnerable
♡ K 7 2   WEST   NORTH   EAST   SOUTH
◇ Q 10 7 4   1♠   2♣   Double   No
♣ 6   ?

What do you do now?

Answer: If partner's double is for penalties, you would pass. Your hand is minimum but not freakish and so there is no sound basis for removing partner's double.

Today, most play the double here as negative, for takeout. If so, rebid 2◇. As long as you do not mislead partner as to your strength, show a second suit before repeating a five-card suit.

♠ A Q 10 6 3   ♠ K J 2
♡ K 7 2   N   ♡ A 6 4 3
◇ Q 10 7 4   W   E   ◇ K J 8 3
♣ 6   S   ♣ 8 4

Against 4♠, North leads the ace of clubs and continues with the king of clubs. How should declarer play?

```
            ♠ 4
            ♡ J 9 8
            ◇ A 6 5
            ♣ A K J 10 5 2
♠ A Q 10 6 3                      ♠ K J 2
♡ K 7 2          N                ♡ A 6 4 3
◇ Q 10 7 4    W     E             ◇ K J 8 3
♣ 6              S                ♣ 8 4
            ♠ 9 8 7 5
            ♡ Q 10 5
            ◇ 9 2
            ♣ Q 9 7 3
```

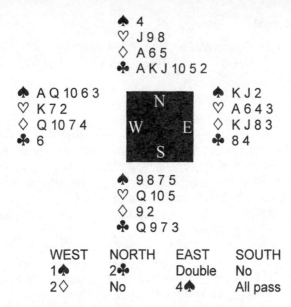

WEST	NORTH	EAST	SOUTH
1♠	2♣	Double	No
2◇	No	4♠	All pass

'What's the problem?' you ask, 'Ruff the club, draw trumps and knock out the ace of diamonds.' Draw trumps? Aye, there's the rub. What if trumps are 4-1? Having ruffed, you are down to four trumps and if you draw four rounds, they cash a heap of clubs on coming in with the ace of diamonds.

'All right,' you reply, 'I ruff the club and knock out the ◇A first.'

That's fine if they promise to take the ◇A on the first round or if the ◇A is doubleton but suppose the layout is as above and North ducks the first diamond. If you lead a second diamond, North wins and can give South a diamond ruff. You have now lost three tricks and there is an inevitable heart loser.

'Inevitable loser' provides the clue. Instead of ruffing the second club, discard the ♡2, a 'loser-on-loser' play. If a third club is played, dummy can take the ruff. Then draw trumps and knock out the ◇A. Taking the ruff in the short trump hand is a useful strategy to retain control in trumps. If North switches at trick three, you win and follow the same route.

The risk in discarding on the second club is that spades are 3-2 with diamonds 4-1 and a diamond ruff ensues. Since they did not find the diamond switch at trick 2, the risk is worth taking.

28. You, West, hold:

♠ K Q 8 5   Dealer West : Nil vulnerable
♡ A Q 3   WEST   NORTH   EAST   SOUTH
◇ Q 10 5 2   ?
♣ A 6

What should West open?

Answer: Playing 1NT as 12-14 and 2NT as 20-22, 4-4-3-2 patterns in the 15-19 range start with one of the four-card suits. It will not hurt to open the cheaper four-card suit but as you are likely to finish in no-trumps, the less information you give to the opponents the better. Your first priority is to locate a major fit and with 4-4 in the majors, always open 1♡. With a major and a minor, start with the major as long as you have a stopper in each of the other suits. Then you can rebid no-trumps even if there is a suit overcall by an opponent. Here it is sound to open 1♠.

If you have an unguarded suit, it is better to start with the cheaper four-card suit. Then if there is an overcall in your weak suit, you will not mislead partner as to your suit lengths if you are forced to rebid in your second suit.

♠ K Q 8 5   Dealer West : Nil vulnerable
♡ A Q 3   WEST   NORTH   EAST   SOUTH
◇ Q 10 5 2   1♠   4♣   4♠   No
♣ A 6   ?

What do you do now?

Answer: You have a strong opening and partner may also have a strong hand, making slam likely. On the other hand, the pre-empt may have forced partner into bidding 4♠ with shaded values. It is better to be conservative after a pre-empt. Pass.

♠ K Q 8 5   ♠ J 10 7 4 2
♡ A Q 3   ♡ 8 5 2
◇ Q 10 5 2   ◇ A K 9 4
♣ A 6   ♣ 7

Against 4♠, North leads the ◇7. Plan the play.

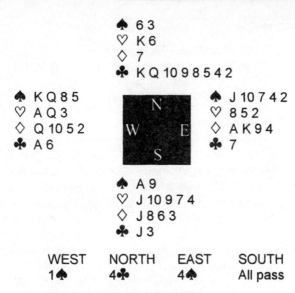

```
              ♠ 6 3
              ♡ K 6
              ♢ 7
              ♣ K Q 10 9 8 5 4 2

♠ K Q 8 5                      ♠ J 10 7 4 2
♡ A Q 3          N             ♡ 8 5 2
♢ Q 10 5 2   W       E         ♢ A K 9 4
♣ A 6            S             ♣ 7

              ♠ A 9
              ♡ J 10 9 7 4
              ♢ J 8 6 3
              ♣ J 3
```

WEST	NORTH	EAST	SOUTH
1♠	4♣	4♠	All pass

6♠ is hopeless but you can hardly blame East for bidding 4♠. That will be challenge enough.

The lead in an unbid suit by a pre-empter is almost always a singleton and you should judge the ♢7 lead accordingly. The danger is that the defence scores a diamond ruff if South has the ace of trumps. That makes two losers and you could lose two more if the ♡K is offside.

There is a neat solution. Win the diamond lead in hand and cash the ace of clubs. Ruff the ♣6 in dummy with an honour (just in case North started with nine clubs) and lead a low trump. If South rises with the ace and plays a diamond, North can ruff but is endplayed if he has no more trumps. A heart return or a ruff-and-discard with a club secures your game.

If North does exit with a spade after ruffing the diamond, cash the ace of hearts, cross to dummy in diamonds and lead a heart to your queen. If South started with the ♡K, you are home and if North has it and a 3-2-1-7 pattern, North with nothing but clubs left will have to give you a ruff-and-discard on winning with the ♡K. A similar line works on the actual deal if you win the diamond lead and play a trump at trick two.

29. You, West, hold:

♠ A K Q 8 7 5 2 Dealer West : Both vulnerable
♡ K
◇ 10 9 5 2 | WEST | NORTH | EAST | SOUTH |
♣ J | ? | | | |

What should West open?

Answer: The choice is between 1♠ and 4♠. The pre-empt would have many adherents as it makes life very tough for the opponents. If you do elect to pre-empt with a strong hand, make sure you start with a game bid. In third or fourth seat, this would be a clearcut 4♠ opening.

To open 1♠ leaves slam options open. It is not hard to envisage partner passing 4♠ with slam laydown. Perhaps something like:

   ♠ x x   ♡ A Q J 10 x   ◇ A x x   ♣ K x x

We have no quarrel with 4♠ but when this hand arose in the 1979 European Ladies' Teams, 1♠ was the choice.

♠ A K Q 8 7 5 2 Dealer West : Both vulnerable

♡ K	WEST	NORTH	EAST	SOUTH
◇ 10 9 5 2	1♠	Double	2♡	3♣
♣ J	?			

What should you do now?

Answer: With a suit quality of 10+, insist on your suit as trumps. Suit Quality Test: Add the honour cards in your long suit to the number of cards in the suit. The answer is the suit quality of that suit. Seven spades + three honours = SQ10. Bid 4♠.

♠ A K Q 8 7 5 2   ♠ J 10
♡ K   ♡ Q J 10 8 5
◇ 10 9 5 2   ◇ 7 4 3
♣ J   ♣ A 10 8

Against 4♠, North leads the ♣3. Declarer wins with the ace and leads a heart to the king and North's ace. To your surprise and pleasure, North returns the ♣5. Plan the play.

```
                    ♠ 9
                    ♡ A 9 6 4 3
                    ◊ K Q 8 6
                    ♣ Q 5 3
♠ A K Q 8 7 5 2                         ♠ J 10
♡ K                                     ♡ Q J 10 8 5
◊ 10 9 5 2        W  N  E  S            ◊ 7 4 3
♣ J                                     ♣ A 10 8
                    ♠ 6 4 3
                    ♡ 7 2
                    ◊ A J
                    ♣ K 9 7 6 4 2
```

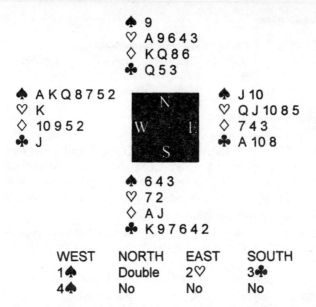

WEST	NORTH	EAST	SOUTH
1♠	Double	2♡	3♣
4♠	No	No	No

East's 2♡ might raise a few eyebrows today. It certainly did not in 1979.

Declarer, Nicola Smith of Great Britain, could see four losers on top with no way to eliminate any of them quickly. Impassively, she took the ace of clubs and led the five of hearts to her king. North won and, not perceiving the danger, continued with the five of clubs. As clubs could not provide enough tricks to defeat 4♠, a switch to diamonds was indicated. Also, after North's double and ♣3 lead, South should discourage clubs.

Declarer capitalised on her good fortune. She ruffed the club, crossed to dummy's ♠J and cashed the ♡Q on which a diamond was discarded. When the ♡J was led, South ruffed and declarer over-ruffed. A trump to the ten drew South's last trump and a second diamond discard on the ♡10 landed the game.

At the other table, the play was the same for the first three tricks. The French West erred by playing two rounds of trumps before reverting to hearts. When South ruffed the third heart, the contract was doomed.

Not surprisingly, Nicola went on to win many honours, including three world championships to date.

30. You, West, hold:

♠ A K 10 9 7	Dealer West : Nil vulnerable			
♡ A K Q 10	WEST	NORTH	EAST	SOUTH
◇ 6 3	1♠	No	2◇	No
♣ 7 3	?			

What should West bid now?

Answer: You have a strong hand, certainly enough for game opposite a two-over-one response, but there is no need to jump. Change of suit is forcing after a two-level response and it is better to reserve the jump to 3♡ either for hands close to slam values, 19+ points, or for a 5-5 pattern. Bid 2♡.

♠ A K 10 9 7	WEST	NORTH	EAST	SOUTH
♡ A K Q 10	1♠	No	2◇	No
◇ 6 3	2♡	No	4♠	No
♣ 7 3	?			

What should West do now?

Answer: Partner's jump to game indicates a hand of around opening strength with three-card or better support for spades. You are much stronger than you might be, since your 2♡ rebid promised no extra strength. You have five losers and that should be enough for a slam opposite the seven or so losers expected in partner's hand.

You could ask for aces with 4NT but your club holding is a worry. Partner could have strength in diamonds and spades with no club control either. Bid 5♡, a cue bid showing the ace of hearts and simultaneously denying the minor suit aces.

♠ A K 10 9 7		♠ Q J 8
♡ A K Q 10	N	♡ 8 7 2
◇ 6 3	W E	◇ A J 8 7 4
♣ 7 3	S	♣ A J

You finish in 6♠ and North leads the king of clubs.
Can you find a way home in this slam?

```
                    ♠ 6 3
                    ♡ 9 4
                    ◇ Q 10 9 5
                    ♣ K Q 10 8 4
♠ A K 10 9 7                        ♠ Q J 8
♡ A K Q 10          ┌─────┐         ♡ 8 7 2
◇ 6 3               │  N  │         ◇ A J 8 7 4
♣ 7 3            W  │     │  E      ♣ A J
                    │  S  │
                    └─────┘
                    ♠ 5 4 2
                    ♡ J 6 5 3
                    ◇ K 2
                    ♣ 9 6 5 2
```

WEST	NORTH	EAST	SOUTH
1♠	No	2◇	No
2♡	No	4♠	No
5♡	No	6♠	All pass

Any decent partner would have put down a dummy with six diamonds and doubletons in hearts and clubs. That would have made the play a lot easier. Still, never say die.

With an inescapable diamond loser, you will have to eliminate the club loser. There is only one way to do that: discard dummy's club on the fourth round of hearts and then ruff your club in dummy. As necessity is the mother of invention, the cards will have to lie perfectly for this plan to work.

Start by drawing precisely two rounds of trumps. They break 3-2. That's a good start. Then play off two top hearts. If the jack has dropped, continue hearts. If the player with four or five hearts holds the last trump, you are on the road to success.

When the jack fails to drop in two rounds, pray that the hearts are 4-2. If hearts are 3-3, you cannot succeed. The thirteenth heart would be ruffed and you cannot escape a second loser. When all follow low to the first two rounds of hearts, cross to the ace of diamonds and lead a heart from dummy. When South plays low, finesse your ten. When it wins, cash your last heart and throw dummy's club loser, ruff the club in dummy and do your best to avoid dancing a jig around the table.

31. You, West, hold:

♠ A 2
♡ K J 8 7 2
♢ A 6 4
♣ 7 6 3

Dealer West : North-South vulnerable

WEST	NORTH	EAST	SOUTH
?			

What do you do as dealer?

Answer: Playing 1NT 12-14, you need to decide how to handle this strength with a 5-3-3-2 and a five-card major. Many prefer 1♡ but the number of proponents for 1NT is growing.

After 1♡ : 1♠ you can raise spades with three-card support while with your actual pattern, you have to choose between rebidding 2♡ or a three-card minor.

♠ A 2
♡ K J 8 7 2
♢ A 6 4
♣ 7 6 3

Dealer West : North-South vulnerable

WEST	NORTH	EAST	SOUTH
1♡	No	2NT	Double

2NT is the Jacoby Convention. What does South's double mean?

Answer: The Jacoby 2NT response is a game-force (13+ points) with 4+ support for opener's suit and no singleton or void.

South's double is for takeout, showing a shortage in hearts and support for the other suits.

What action do you take?

Answer: The standard answer, chosen at the table, is 4♡. In Jacoby this shows a minimum opening with no short suit. If playing 5-card majors, there is a good case for the 3NT rebid to show a modest 5-3-3-2. Responder can then pass with a 4-3-3-3 pattern.

♠ A 2   ♠ K J 9
♡ K J 8 7 2   ♡ A Q 6 4
♢ A 6 4   ♢ 10 9 8
♣ 7 6 3   ♣ Q J 2

South doubles 4♡ and all pass. North leads ♢5. Plan the play.

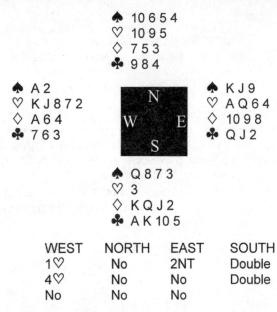

```
                    ♠ 10 6 5 4
                    ♡ 10 9 5
                    ◇ 7 5 3
                    ♣ 9 8 4
    ♠ A 2                              ♠ K J 9
    ♡ K J 8 7 2        N               ♡ A Q 6 4
    ◇ A 6 4       W         E          ◇ 10 9 8
    ♣ 7 6 3            S               ♣ Q J 2
                    ♠ Q 8 7 3
                    ♡ 3
                    ◇ K Q J 2
                    ♣ A K 10 5
```

WEST	NORTH	EAST	SOUTH
1♡	No	2NT	Double
4♡	No	No	Double
No	No	No	

3NT would have been easier. In 4♡ you are faced with two diamond losers and two club losers. In view of the two doubles, you can be very confident that South holds almost every missing high card and so three club losers are more likely than not.

To have any chance, you need to produce a third spade trick to eliminate one diamond loser. As South is an overwhelming favourite to hold the ♠Q, how do you score three spade tricks?

The answer is via 'a backward finesse'. Cross to the ♡A and lead the ♠J. If South plays low, so do you. If South plays the ♠Q, you capture it and finesse the ♠9 on the way back. If North has the ♠10, you are in business.

To avoid three club losers you need to set up an endplay against South. Start by ducking the first diamond. Win the diamond continuation, cross to the ♡A and lead the ♠J as above. On the third round of spades, discard your diamond loser. Ruff a diamond in hand and draw the missing trumps. With only hearts and clubs left in your hands, lead a club to dummy's queen. South wins but must give you a club trick or a ruff-and-discard, which is just as good.

32. You, West, hold:

♠ 9 4 3   Dealer West : Both vulnerable
♥ A 6 2
♦ A K 6 4 2
♣ J 4

WEST	NORTH	EAST	SOUTH
?			

What action should West take?

Answer: With 12-14 points and a 5-3-3-2 pattern with the five-card suit a minor, it is normal to start with 1NT.

♠ 9 4 3
♥ A 6 2
♦ A K 6 4 2
♣ J 4

WEST	NORTH	EAST	SOUTH
1NT	No	2◇ (1)	2♠
?			

(1) Transfer to hearts

What should West do now?

Answer: The transfer shows 5+ hearts but East may have a very weak hand. Had South passed, you would have bid 2♥ but over 2♠ there is no obligation to bid and so you should pass.

♠ 9 4 3
♥ A 6 2
♦ A K 6 4 2
♣ J 4

WEST	NORTH	EAST	SOUTH
1NT	No	2◇	2♠
No	No	2NT	No
?			

Now what?

Answer: 2NT invites game. You are minimum but have three-card heart support. Bid 3♥. North passes and East raises to 4♥. This is passed back to North who doubles for penalties.

♠ 9 4 3   ♠ Q 7
♥ A 6 2   ♥ K 10 8 4 3
♦ A K 6 4 2   ♦ 8 3
♣ J 4   ♣ A K 8 2

North leads ♠2, low from dummy and South's ♠A wins. South cashes ♠K (♠5 from North) and switches to ◇Q. Plan the play.

```
            ♠ 10 5 2
            ♡ Q J 9 7 5
            ◇ 9 5
            ♣ Q 10 9
```

```
♠ 9 4 3                          ♠ Q 7
♡ A 6 2                          ♡ K 10 8 4 3
◇ A K 6 4 2                      ◇ 8 3
♣ J 4                            ♣ A K 8 2
```

```
            ♠ A K J 8 6
            ♡ - - -
            ◇ Q J 10 7
            ♣ 7 6 5 3
```

WEST	NORTH	EAST	SOUTH
1NT	No	2◇	2♠
No	No	2NT	No
3♡	No	4♡	No
No	Double	All pass	

In view of South's strength in spades and diamonds, North's double must be based on a trump stack. In all probability, North has all five missing trumps.

You cannot afford to start on trumps but dummy's spot cards may be enough to counter North's trumps. Given the ♠2 lead, North figures to hold three spades. Take the ◇A and ruff a spade in dummy. With five hearts and three spades, North can hold only five cards in the minors. Pray that these are 3-2 and not 4-1. As you have greater length in diamonds than clubs, the odds favour North holding three clubs and two diamonds.

Continue with ♣A, ♣K and ruff a club with the ♡6. When that survives, play the ◇K and lead a third diamond. If North ruffs low, say ♡5, over-ruff with ♡8 and ruff your last club with the ♡A. Lead a trump and if North inserts an honour, play the ♡4, leaving dummy with the K-10 over North's Q-9 or J-9.

If North ruffs the third diamond with the ♡J, say, discard your club loser. When North leads a trump, win cheaply, play off the ace of trumps and again dummy has a tenace over North.

33. You, East, hold:

♠ A J 9 7   Dealer East : Both vulnerable
♡ Q J 10 9   **WEST**   **NORTH**   **EAST**   **SOUTH**
♢ 4   ?
♣ A Q 4 3

What would you do as dealer?

Answer: When opening with a 4-4-4-1 pattern, choose the middle suit if you hold a black singleton and open the suit below the singleton if you have a red singleton. That provides maximum flexibility in showing your suits. Open 1♣.

♠ A J 9 7   Dealer East : Both vulnerable
♡ Q J 10 9   **WEST**   **NORTH**   **EAST**   **SOUTH**
♢ 4   1♣   No
♣ A Q 4 3   1♡   Double   ?

What action do you take now?

Answer: Had North passed, you would have raised to 3♡, Should North's double deflect you from that course? Unless your system dictates otherwise, make the same bid you would have made without interference. You should have faith in your system, so why let the actions of the opponents dictate a change in your good methods?

There is no value in introducing the spades and redouble should show a strong hand but with a shortage in partner's suit. The function of the redouble is to let partner know that your side has the majority of points, that the hand is probably a misfit and that a penalty double of their bid may be attractive.

2♡ would be too timid with 14 HCP plus a singleton. Bid 3♡.

♠ 8   ♠ A J 9 7
♡ K 8 5 4 3   ♡ Q J 10 9
♢ A 6 5 2   ♢ 4
♣ 8 6 2   ♣ A Q 4 3

Against 4♡, North leads the ace of hearts, followed by the two of hearts, South following both times. Plan the play.

```
                        ♠ K Q 10 5
                        ♡ A 2
                        ◇ K Q 10 9 7
                        ♣ 10 7
        ♠ 8                                    ♠ A J 9 7
        ♡ K 8 5 4 3            N               ♡ Q J 10 9
        ◇ A 6 5 2        W           E         ◇ 4
        ♣ 8 6 2                                ♣ A Q 4 3
                              S
                        ♠ 6 4 3 2
                        ♡ 7 6
                        ◇ J 8 3
                        ♣ K J 9 5
```

WEST	NORTH	EAST	SOUTH
		1♣	No
1♡	Double	3♡	No
4♡	No	No	No

You have 21 HCP and because of the double, North figures to hold most of the missing 19. Without the trump lead you could have cross-ruffed in diamonds and spades but after North's trump leads, dummy has only two trumps while you have three diamond losers.

If the club finesse is on, you will lose just one heart, one diamond and one club. Therefore assume the ♣K is offside. If clubs are 3-3, the thirteenth club will allow you to discard a diamond and all will be well. Therefore assume the clubs are not 3-3. Is there anything else?

There is no rush to tackle clubs. If the ♣K is with North or if clubs are 3-3, that will still be so in two tricks time. The late Ron Andersen, one of the greatest USA players, won the second trick in hand and led the ♠8. North naturally played the queen and that was enough for Andersen.

He took the ♠A and returned the ♠J, discarding a club from hand. North won and switched to the ♣10. Declarer played dummy's ace and exited with the ♠9. He discarded the ♣8 and the ♠7 was now a winner in dummy for a diamond discard.

34. You, West, hold:

♠ K Q 10 6 3   Dealer North : North-South vulnerable
♡ 7 4   WEST   NORTH   EAST   SOUTH
♢ A 7 6   1♡   No   No
♣ K J 10   ?

What do you do in the pass-out seat?

Answer: There is great urgency to bid here, else the opponents buy the contract cheaply. A suit bid can be as weak as 7 points and there is no suit quality requirement for an overcall here.

On that basis you have a very strong hand and a very good suit for a mere 1♠ overcall. To jump to 2♠ would express the strength (weak jump overcalls are not recommended in the balancing seat) but that would indicate a six-card suit. Double also includes this strength but what if partner replies 2♣ or 2♢? You would not be happy to pass that with such good spades but to double and remove partner's bid to 2♠ would imply a 5-6 loser hand of 16 points or so. Your best move is to bid 1♠.

♠ K Q 10 6 3   WEST   NORTH   EAST   SOUTH
♡ 7 4   1♡   No   No
♢ A 7 6   1♠   2♡   3♡   No
♣ K J 10   ?

What is 3 ♡ all about? What do you bid?

Answer: 3♡ is a strong raise to 3♠ based on high cards. As you are much better than you might be for 1♠, you should bid 4♠.

♠ K Q 10 6 3   ♠ J 9 7 2
♡ 7 4   ♡ Q 5 2
♢ A 7 6   ♢ K Q 8
♣ K J 10   ♣ A 7 6

Against 4♠, North cashes ♡A, ♡K and leads the ♡J. South ruffs but you over-ruff. North captures your ♠K with the ♠A, on which South discards the ♣2. North exits with the ♠5, South discarding the ♣3. How do you plan the play?

```
                  ♠ A 8 5
                  ♡ A K J 10 6 3
                  ◇ J 10 9
                  ♣ 5
  ♠ K Q 10 6 3                      ♠ J 9 7 2
  ♡ 7 4                             ♡ Q 5 2
  ◇ A 7 6                           ◇ K Q 8
  ♣ K J 10                          ♣ A 7 6
                  ♠ 4
                  ♡ 9 8
                  ◇ 5 4 3 2
                  ♣ Q 9 8 4 3 2
```

WEST	NORTH	EAST	SOUTH
	1♡	No	No
1♠	2♡	3♡	No
4♠	No	No	No

After three rounds of hearts and ♠K, taken by the ace, South pitching ♣2, North exited with a spade, South discarding ♣3.

Naturally you draw North's last trump and the instinctive move then is to play North for the ♣Q. After all, North bid twice and South could not reply to North's opening bid. In addition, South has discarded two clubs. All the clues point to the ♣Q with North.

There is no rush to play the clubs. Declarer, the late Lewis Ellison, one of Britain's best players in the immediate post-war era, found the best move, playing off three rounds of diamonds first, a 'discovery play'. Finishing in hand, he led the ♣J. When North fumbled and hesitated, Lewis inquired:

"Which half of your singleton club do you intend to play?",

How did he know? By *counting*. North had shown up early on with six hearts and three spades. When he also followed to three rounds of diamonds, he could not hold more than one club. The jack of clubs was played to test North's ethics. North failed.

Naturally, when North follows with any club other than the queen, West overtakes the ♣J with dummy's ♣A and finesses the ♣10 on the way back.

35. You, East, hold:

```
♠ A 7        Dealer West : Nil vulnerable
♡ J 5 4 3    WEST    NORTH    EAST    SOUTH
♢ K 3        1♢      No       ?
♣ Q J 10 9 3
```

What do you respond?

Answer: If your reply is 'Two clubs, what's the problem?' we are in wholehearted agreement with you. Provided you are strong enough to show both suits, bid your longest suit first. 1♡ would be right only if too weak for a two-over-one response.

```
♠ A 7        Dealer West : Nil vulnerable
♡ J 5 4 3    WEST    NORTH    EAST    SOUTH
♢ K 3        1♢      No       2♣      No
♣ Q J 10 9 3 2NT     No       ?
```

How do you continue?

Answer: Playing a 12-14 1NT opening, 2NT shows 15+ points. You have enough for game but 3NT is not necessarily best. West could hold four hearts. Explore that possibility by bidding 3♡.

```
♠ A 7        WEST    NORTH    EAST    SOUTH
♡ J 5 4 3    1♢      No       2♣      No
♢ K 3        2NT     No       3♡      No
♣ Q J 10 9 3 3♠      No       ?
```

What now?

Answer: 3♠ expresses concern about spades for 3NT. As you have a spade stopper, bid 3NT.

```
        ♠ 10 9 4 3              ♠ A 7
        ♡ A K 6        N        ♡ J 5 4 3
        ♢ A Q 9 7    W   E      ♢ K 3
        ♣ K 4          S        ♣ Q J 10 9 3
```

Against 3NT, North leads the ♠6. Plan West's play?

```
                    ♠ K J 8 6 2
                    ♡ Q 10 2
                    ◇ 6 4 2
                    ♣ A 2
♠ 10 9 4 3                              ♠ A 7
♡ A K 6             N                   ♡ J 5 4 3
◇ A Q 9 7       W       E               ◇ K 3
♣ K 4               S                   ♣ Q J 10 9 3
                    ♠ Q 5
                    ♡ 9 8 7
                    ◇ J 10 8 5
                    ♣ 8 7 6 5
```

WEST	NORTH	EAST	SOUTH
1◇	No	2♣	No
2NT	No	3♡	No
3♠	No	3NT	All pass

There are six tricks on top and the clubs will provide the extra needed. The snag is that the opponents have attacked your weak suit. Is there any hope other than a 4-3 break in spades?

There are four cards higher than the ♠6 between you and dummy. The Rule of Eleven thus tells you that South can hold only one card higher than the ♠6.

That card must be an honour, for from a suit headed by the K-Q-J North would have led the king. If this assumption is correct, you can guarantee your game by playing the ♠A at trick one.

If the spades are 4-3, the opponents can take no more than three spades and the ♣A. If North has six spades and South a singleton honour, your remaining ♠10-9-4 will stop the run of the spades. If South began with honour-doubleton and unblocks the honour under the ace, your ♠10-9-4 is again a stopper. If South retains the honour, the suit is blocked. South can cash the honour after coming in with the ♣A but there is no way to reach the North hand to cash the remaining spades. If North overtakes South's honour, your spades hold the fort.

36. You, West, hold:

♠ K J 7   Dealer North : East-West vulnerable
♡ - - -

	WEST	NORTH	EAST	SOUTH
◇ A K J 10 9 6		1♡	No	2♡
♣ Q 9 8 6	?			

What action do you take?

Answer: Your rational choices are Double, 3◇, 4◇ or 5◇. Of these the most attractive is 3◇. At this vulnerability you are bound to have a good hand to enter the bidding at the three-level and so there is no need to jump to 4◇. To jump to 5◇ is even less appealing. They may not be bidding to game and even if they do, 5◇ doubled might prove very expensive.

Double would appeal more if you held four spades. If you did double and partner bid any number of spades, you would not be comfortable staying there. If you intend to double and remove a spade bid to diamonds, you may as well bid the diamonds at once. That will point the way to the right lead if North ends up as declarer.

♠ K J 7
♡ - - -

	WEST	NORTH	EAST	SOUTH
		1♡	No	2♡
◇ A K J 10 9 6	3◇	4♡	5◇	No
♣ Q 9 8 6	?			

What now?

Answer: Your heart void is a significant asset and partner will have a decent hand to bid 5◇ at this vulnerability. Although slam may well be on, you have too many gaps and too little information about partner's hand to bid six. Pass 5◇.

♠ K J 7   ♠ 6 4 2
♡ - - -   ♡ J 10 8
◇ A K J 10 9 6   ◇ Q 8
♣ Q 9 8 6   ♣ A K 5 4 2

North leads the ♣7 against 5◇. Plan your play.

```
                    ♠ A Q 9
                    ♡ A 9 7 6 5 4
                    ◇ 7 5 4
                    ♣ 7
♠ K J 7                                   ♠ 6 4 2
♡ - - -             N                     ♡ J 10 8
◇ A K J 10 9 6    W   E                   ◇ Q 8
♣ Q 9 8 6           S                     ♣ A K 5 4 2
                    ♠ 10 8 5 3
                    ♡ K Q 3 2
                    ◇ 3 2
                    ♣ J 10 3
```

WEST	NORTH	EAST	SOUTH
	1♡	No	2♡
3◇	4♡	5◇	All pass

It is not hard to pick the opening club lead as a singleton. If South does hold ♣J-10-3, the club suit is blocked and is worth only four tricks. To prevent a club ruff, drawing trumps might seem sensible but if you do, you are relying on South holding either ♠A or ♠Q.

West, Guglielmo Siniscalco, wanted better odds. Winning the lead in dummy, he led the ♡J. South covered by ♡Q, ruffed *high* by West. After ◇6 to dummy's eight, declarer continued with the ♡10. South played ♡K and West ruffed. Another trump to dummy was followed by the ♡8. When South did not cover, declarer discarded the ♣8. North won but could not successfully attack spades. He exited with a trump won by declarer who could now cash the clubs, thanks to his jettison play in clubs. He discarded two spades and conceded a spade to the opponents.

Declarer was playing for North to have either two of the top heart honours, or one honour and the ♡9, or South the ♠Q. Even this fine plan can be improved to cater for a 4-1 trump split. Win the club lead in hand and lead ◇6 to ◇8. The ♡J is covered by the ♡Q and ruffed. Cross to the ◇Q. If trumps are 3-2, lead ♡10 – ♡K – ruff, draw the last trump, cross to ♣K and lead ♡8, ditching the ♣8 whether South covers or not. If trumps are 4-1, play a spade to the jack (after ◇Q) and hope South has the ♠Q.

37. You, West, hold:

♠ K Q 10 9 6 4   Dealer South : Nil vulnerable
♡ 7   WEST   NORTH   EAST   SOUTH
◇ 9 8 6 2   1♣
♣ K 3   ?

What should West do?

Answer: You can make a case for 1♠, 2♠ (weak jump overcall) or 3♠. You do little harm to the opponents' auction with 1♠ and so 2♠ weak appeals more, but the red-blooded bid is 3♠. A 6-4 pattern has as much playing strength as a seven-card suit and if West held a 7-1-3-2 pattern, 3♠ would be the popular choice.

Another useful guide is the Suit Quality Test (see Problem #29). As long as the strength is adequate, you can overcall in your suit for the same number of tricks as its suit quality. As the SQ of the spades is 9, you can bid for nine tricks. Bid 3♠.

♠ K Q 10 9 6 4   WEST   NORTH   EAST   SOUTH
♡ 7   1♣
◇ 9 8 6 2   3♠   Double   4◇   4♡
♣ K 3   ?

North's double is for takeout. How do you take 4◇?
What do you do now?

Answer: After the takeout double, South is quite likely to become declarer. Partners often use this opportunity to make a lead-directing bid and 4◇ shows strength in diamonds without necessarily having length there. As you cannot be sure of East's intentions, you should pass. It would be insensitive to bid 5◇.

♠ K Q 10 9 6 4		♠ 8 2
♡ 7	N	♡ 9 6 2
◇ 9 8 6 2	W E	◇ A K Q 7
♣ K 3	S	♣ 7 6 5 2

4♡ is passed to East who bids 4♠, passed out. North leads the four of clubs to South's ace. South returns the ♣J. Plan the play.

```
                    ♠ 7 5
                    ♡ A Q 10 8 3
                    ◇ 10 5 4
                    ♣ Q 8 4

    ♠ K Q 10 9 6 4          ♠ 8 2
    ♡ 7            N        ♡ 9 6 2
    ◇ 9 8 6 2   W     E     ◇ A K Q 7
    ♣ K 3          S        ♣ 7 6 5 2

                    ♠ A J 3
                    ♡ K J 5 4
                    ◇ J 3
                    ♣ A J 10 9
```

WEST	NORTH	EAST	SOUTH
			1♣
3♠	Double	4◇	4♡
No	No	4♠	All pass

As South bid 4♡ despite the 4◇ bid, East suspected a singleton spade with an opponent and bid 4♠. As the cards lie, 4♡ can be beaten, thanks to the location of the ♣K.

A penalty double of 4♠ by South would be forgivable but when the deal arose, 4♠ was passed out. Declarer was America's Billy Eisenberg who has won a number of world championships.

After a low club lead to the ace and the ♣J returned, declarer won and crossed to the ace of diamonds in order to lead a spade. When South played low, declarer won with the ♠K. Finessing the ♠9 or ♠10 would have worked, but this was a risky move. While South as the opener was highly likely to hold the ♠A, the ♠J could easily have been with North.

Had declarer continued with a diamond to dummy to lead a second spade, the defence could have prevailed. South takes the ♠A and leads a heart. North wins and gives South a diamond ruff. Foreseeing this danger, declarer executed a 'scissors coup' by leading the ♡7 at trick five. On regaining the lead, declarer entered dummy with a diamond and led a second spade. South could win but there was no entry to North for the diamond ruff.

38. You, West, hold:

♠ K 2   Dealer West : Both vulnerable
♡ J 9 7 5 4 3   **WEST   NORTH   EAST   SOUTH**
◇ A Q   1♡   No   2NT   No
♣ Q 6 5   ?

2NT is the Jacoby Convention. What does that mean?

Answer: The 2NT Jacoby response is forcing to game (usually 13+ points) with 4+ support for opener's suit and no singleton or void. A new suit by opener at the three-level then shows a singleton or void in the suit bid.

What action do you take with no singleton or void?

Answer: 3NT shows extra strength but no extra length in the suit opened. Repeating the suit at the three-level shows extra length and extra strength. Here you jump to 4♡ to show a minimum opening with no singleton or void. As you did not open 1NT (12-14), 4♡ logically shows at least a five-card suit.

♠ K 2   **WEST   NORTH   EAST   SOUTH**
♡ J 9 7 5 4 3   1♡   No   2NT   No
◇ A Q   4♡   No   5♣   No
♣ Q 6 5   ?

What does 5♣ mean? What do you do?

Answer: 5♣ is a cue-bid showing slam interest (despite the weakness shown by your 4♡ bid). It promises the ♣A and denies the ♠A. As you have the ◇A and second round control in spades, you should jump to 6♡.

♠ K 2   ♠ Q J 10
♡ J 9 7 5 4 3   ♡ A Q 8 2
◇ A Q   ◇ K J 5 4
♣ Q 6 5   ♣ A K

Against 6♡ North starts with the ace of spades and continues with the nine of spades. How would you plan the play?

```
            ♠ A 9 5 4
            ♡ K 10 6
            ◇ 8 3 2
            ♣ 9 4 2
♠ K 2                          ♠ Q J 10
♡ J 9 7 5 4 3     N            ♡ A Q 8 2
◇ A Q          W     E         ◇ K J 5 4
♣ Q 6 5           S            ♣ A K
            ♠ 8 7 6 3
            ♡ - - -
            ◇ 10 9 7 6
            ♣ J 10 8 7 3
```

WEST	NORTH	EAST	SOUTH
1♡	No	2NT	No
4♡	No	5♣	No
6♡	No	No	No

You should sympathise with East's dilemma. Had East bid 4NT
Roman Key Card Blackwood over 4♡, you would have stopped in
5♡ as two key cards are missing. However, if you had shown two
key cards, East might have bid 6♡ only to have the opponents
cash the first two spades. As you are more likely to hold the ♡K
than the ♠K, the cue-bidding sequence is sensible.

Note that you gain nothing by cue-bidding 5◇ over 5♣. With no
spade control, East would sign off in 5♡ and you would bid 6♡.
As you would welcome a diamond lead, jump to 6♡ over 5♣.

After the ♠A lead and a second spade, your problem is to avoid
a trump loser. With ten trumps missing the king, the odds in favour
of finessing are about 3-1. Playing the ace works only if South has
the ♡K singleton. The finesse works in three cases: when South
holds the ♡10 singleton or ♡6 singleton or a void in hearts.

To cater for North holding all three hearts, lead the ♡J first. If
North plays low, the jack wins and you repeat the finesse. If North
covers with the king, South shows out on the ♡A. You come to
hand in diamonds and finesse against North's ♡10. Leading the
jack first would be unsound if you had fewer than ten trumps.

39. You, West, hold:

♠ 4 2　　　　　Dealer West : Nil vulnerable
♡ A Q 9 7 6 5　WEST　　NORTH　　EAST　　SOUTH
◇ K J 3　　　　1♡　　　No　　　　2◇　　　No
♣ A 4　　　　　?

What should West rebid?

Answer: The three sane choices are 2♡, 3◇ or 3♡. It is always a sound idea to support partner but the expectation for 3◇ would be four-card support. Your three-card support is strong and were your hearts less attractive, 3◇ would be acceptable. Much of the time partner has a 5+ suit when bidding the most distant suit over your opening bid (such as 1◇ : 2♣ also).

Had partner responded 1♠ it would be enough to bid 2♡. You have no useful cards in spades and your diamond holding may or may not produce tricks. After the 2◇ response, however, you are definitely worth 3♡. Partner is highly likely to hold either the ◇A or the ◇Q or both and if so, your diamond honours are sure to be useful. Your jump to 3♡ promises six hearts and is forcing to game after the two-over-one response. If partner bids 3NT, you will pass and if partner bids 3♠ over 3♡, you can bid 3NT as you have a stopper in clubs.

Had partner responded 2♣, your diamond honours are also not certain to be useful. Again 2♡ would be enough, although there are some who would jump to 3♡ nevertheless. As a general guide, be optimistic and pushy in the bidding when you have high cards in partner's suit and tend to be pessimistic and conservative when you lack high cards in partner's suit. A singleton or void in partner's suit is a negative feature.

♠ 4 2　　　　　　　　　　　　　　♠ A K 5
♡ A Q 9 7 6 5　　　　　　　　　♡ 8 4 2
◇ K J 3　　　　　　　　◇ A 10 5 4 2
♣ A 4　　　　　　　　　　　　　　♣ 7 5

North leads the king of clubs against 4♡. Plan the play.

```
                    ♠ 8 7 6
                    ♡ K J 3
                    ◊ 8 6
                    ♣ K Q J 9 2
♠ 4 2                                    ♠ A K 5
♡ A Q 9 7 6 5                            ♡ 8 4 2
◊ K J 3                                  ◊ A 10 5 4 2
♣ A 4                                    ♣ 7 5
```

```
                    ♠ Q J 10 9 3
                    ♡ 10
                    ◊ Q 9 7
                    ♣ 10 8 6 3
```

A respectable line would be to win with the ♣A, cash the ♡A (to guard against a singleton ♡K with North), cross to dummy in spades and lead a heart. That succeeds when hearts are 2-2 or South has the ♡K. When North turns up with three hearts, you are still home if you pick up the ◊Q. Can you improve on that?

Tony Forrester, England's most capped player, demonstrated that, as long as trumps were not 4-0 or spades 7-1 or 8-0, the contract was safe without the need to find the ◊Q. He astounded the kibitzers by the speed of his analysis and play. Like lightning he took the ♣A, cashed the ♡A, crossed to dummy with a spade, played off the second spade winner and ruffed the ♠5. He then exited with a club and waited for the defenders to reduce his losers for him.

Should the ♡K fall singleton or hearts break 2-2, he would make an overtrick but the primary objective was to make the contract. Whoever won the club would have to play a trump (eliminating a loser there) or a diamond (eliminating that loser) or a black suit, giving declarer a ruff-and-discard and so no diamond loser.

If South shows out on the ♡A, there are three trump losers. You must then play North for ◊Q-x-x. If so, you can discard the club loser on the fourth diamond. It would be lucky to find North with this diamond holding but there is no other chance if North has three trump tricks.

40. You, East, hold:

♠ K J 10   Dealer South : East-West vulnerable
♡ Q 8 3
◇ 6 5 4
♣ J 9 8 7

WEST	NORTH	EAST	SOUTH
			No
1♡	No	?	

What do you do with the East cards?

Answer: Opposite a possible four-card 1♡ opening, your 1NT response should be automatic.

Would your answer change if the 1 ♡ opening promised five or more hearts?

Answer: Playing five-card majors, you may raise 1♡ or 1♠ with just three trumps. Even so, you should be discerning with your three-card raises. With a singleton or doubleton in your hand, by all means raise. When you have a 4-3-3-3, prefer the 1NT response unless most of your points are in partner's major.

Furthermore, if your 4-3-3-3 has ten losers, choose the 1NT response. If you raise the major, partner will be anxious to invite or drive to game or to compete further if they intervene. By contrast if you bid 1NT, partner will be reluctant to push too high. With ten losers, you do not want to excite your partner.

Although the single raise to a five-card major is permissible with three trumps, avoid giving a jump raise with only three-card support. Rather change suit and support next round.

Suppose you bid 1NT and opener rebids 3 ♡. What now?

Answer: On the one hand you are minimum for 1NT; on the other you have undisclosed heart support. In general, it is better to raise than to pass when you have undisclosed support.

♠ 9 5   ♠ K J 10
♡ A J 10 9 7 6   ♡ Q 8 3
◇ A 10 2   ◇ 6 5 4
♣ A K   ♣ J 9 8 7

Against 4♡, North leads ◇8. South plays ◇J. Plan West's play.

```
              ♠ A 6 3 2
              ♡ 2
              ◇ 9 8 3
              ♣ Q 10 5 4 3
♠ 9 5
♡ A J 10 9 7 6                    ♠ K J 10
◇ A 10 2          N              ♡ Q 8 3
♣ A K          W     E           ◇ 6 5 4
                  S              ♣ J 9 8 7
              ♠ Q 8 7 4
              ♡ K 5 4
              ◇ K Q J 7
              ♣ 6 2
```

WEST	NORTH	EAST	SOUTH
			No
1♡	No	1NT	No
3♡	No	4♡	All pass

4♡ is not a great contract. It would be markedly better if West held three spades and two diamonds.

As North would lead the king if the diamonds were headed by K-Q, you can place the ◇Q with South. As North's ◇8 opening lead is likely to be a singleton, top of a doubleton or middle from 9-8-x, South probably has all the missing diamond honours. In that case, your path is clear . . . or is it?

Tim Seres, Hungarian born but now resident in Australia and one of the world's great players, had no problems. He took the ace of diamonds and led the ♠5. North played low and Seres rose with dummy's ♠K. He then ran the ♡8, took a second heart finesse and made his game.

How could Seres know the location of the ♠A? As West had two diamonds and a spade to lose, he needed South to hold the ♡K. If South also had the ◇K-Q-J as expected from the opening lead, that comes to 9 HCP. South could not also hold the ♠A, for with 13 HCP he would not have passed as dealer. If you need the cards to lie in a specific way in order to succeed, assume they do lie that way and see what inferences follow.

41. You, West, hold:

♠ K 6   Dealer West : Nil vulnerable
♡ A K 5   WEST   NORTH   EAST   SOUTH
◇ A K 3   ?
♣ Q 6 5 3 2

What would you open with the West cards?

Answer: Playing a 2NT opening as 20-22, you might consider upgrading this hand by one point for the five-card suit and opening 2NT. However, with the clubs so weak, and no bolstering tens or nines, it is better to open only 1♣ with this collection. If partner is too weak to respond, it is hardly likely that you will miss a game.

♠ K 6   Dealer West : Nil vulnerable
♡ A K 5   WEST   NORTH   EAST   SOUTH
◇ A K 3   1♣   1♡   1♠   No
♣ Q 6 5 3 2   ?

What do you bid now?

Answer: In standard Acol, you rebid 2NT with 17-18 and jump to 3NT with 19. This method is inefficient as it consumes so much bidding space when responder has a hand worth slam investigation. The non-forcing nature of the 2NT jump-rebid can also lead to difficulties and guesswork.

An attractive alternative structure when playing a 12-14 1NT is to rebid 1NT with 15-18 (over which responder uses 2♣ to clarify opener's points), jump-rebid to 2NT with 19-20, forcing to game, and open 2NT on 21-22. This simplifies game bidding and increases space for slam-going hands.

♠ K 6   ♠ A Q 7 4
♡ A K 5   ♡ 8 6 2
◇ A K 3   ◇ 8 4 2
♣ Q 6 5 3 2   ♣ K 9 4

North leads the ♡Q against 3NT. How do you plan the play?

```
              ♠ 8 3
              ♡ Q J 10 9 3
              ◇ Q J 5
              ♣ A J 8
♠ K 6                              ♠ A Q 7 4
♡ A K 5        ┌──────────┐        ♡ 8 6 2
◇ A K 3        │    N     │        ◇ 8 4 2
♣ Q 6 5 3 2    │ W     E  │        ♣ K 9 4
               │    S     │
               └──────────┘
              ♠ J 10 9 5 2
              ♡ 7 4
              ◇ 10 9 7 6
              ♣ 10 7
```

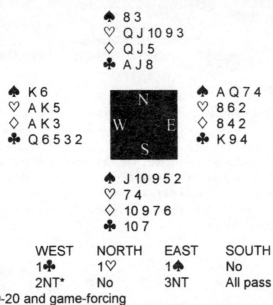

WEST	NORTH	EAST	SOUTH
1♣	1♡	1♠	No
2NT*	No	3NT	All pass

*19-20 and game-forcing

You have seven top tricks and can easily set up another in clubs. The extra trick will have to come from the clubs. At the same time you have to make sure that North is unable to set up and cash enough heart tricks to defeat you.

The declarer was Eddie Kantar, world champion, author, prolific columnist and bridge teacher. His first move was to duck the ♡Q. If the hearts were 4-3 they were no serious threat but if they were 5-2, he wanted to exhaust South's supply.

North continued hearts. Declarer won and led the two of clubs. When North produced the eight, declarer played dummy's nine. South won but had no more hearts. The diamond switch was won by West, who led a second club. No matter when North took the ace, declarer had ten tricks. Declarer's success lay in setting up the clubs by losing a trick to the safe hand, South.

A lesser declarer might have decided that the best chance lay in finding North with the ♣A doubleton. He would lead a low club to the king and a low club back. As the cards lie, this gives North two entries to set up his heart suit before declarer can score a second club trick.

42. You, West, hold:

♠ Q 3 2	Dealer West : Nil vulnerable			
♡ A 2	WEST	NORTH	EAST	SOUTH
◇ A K 4	1♣	No	1◇	No
♣ A 10 9 6 2	?			

What should West rebid?

Answer: Playing standard Acol the rebid would be 2NT, 17-18 points and not forcing. If playing the methods suggested in Problem #41, West would rebid 1NT, showing a balanced hand of 15-18 points. Not only does this save space, but if East has responded on a modest 5-6 count, the bidding can stop at a cheaper level.

After 1♣ : 1◇, 1NT responder's 2♡ or 2♠ is game-forcing and tends to suggest a three-suited hand. After opener's next rebid, responder bids the third suit if convenient. The same applies to 1♣/1◇ : 1♡, 1NT : 2♠.

After 1♣ : 1-suit, 1NT responder's 2♣ rebid is artificial and asks opener to clarify his strength. Opener rebids 2◇ with an absolute minimum (15 points or a 4-3-3-3 16), 2♡/2♠/2NT with 16 points, and a natural bid at the three-level with 17-18 points. After opener's two-level rebid, the bidding can stop below game but a three-level rebid commits the partnership to game. On the above hand, after 1♣ :1◇, 1NT : 2♣ opener would rebid 3♣ to show 17-18 points with a five-card suit.

To sign off in clubs, responder bids 2NT over 1NT to force opener to bid 3♣. Responder passes this with a weak hand and club support, while other bids after 3♣ are natural and force to game. After 1NT, responder's jump-rebid at the three-level is natural and forcing to game.

♠ Q 3 2		♠ A 5
♡ A 2	N	♡ 7 6 5 4
◇ A K 4	W E	◇ Q 7 3 2
♣ A 10 9 6 2	S	♣ K J 8

Against 3NT, North leads the ♠6. How should declarer proceed?

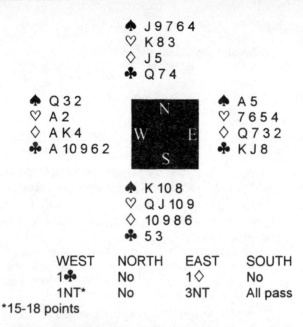

```
                    ♠ J 9 7 6 4
                    ♡ K 8 3
                    ◇ J 5
                    ♣ Q 7 4
    ♠ Q 3 2                          ♠ A 5
    ♡ A 2          N                 ♡ 7 6 5 4
    ◇ A K 4     W       E            ◇ Q 7 3 2
    ♣ A 10 9 6 2       S             ♣ K J 8
                    ♠ K 10 8
                    ♡ Q J 10 9
                    ◇ 10 9 8 6
                    ♣ 5 3
```

WEST	NORTH	EAST	SOUTH
1♣	No	1◇	No
1NT*	No	3NT	All pass

*15-18 points

If you were playing match-pointed pairs, the best move would be to duck the spade lead to score two spade tricks and to try to score as many tricks as possible. Your aim at pairs is not necessarily to make your contract but to outscore the others who hold the same cards as you do.

Here your aim is to make sure of your contract if possible (the normal strategy at rubber bridge or at teams). Start by counting your sure tricks. You have seven: one in each major, three diamonds and two in clubs. The extra two can come from clubs although you may have to lose a trick in the process.

What could go wrong if you duck the spade? If North has the ♠K you score an extra trick. If South takes the ♠K and returns a spade, you have an extra trick. The problem arises if South wins the ♠K and shifts to hearts. Now you could lose five tricks (one spade, one club and three hearts) if you mispick the clubs.

3NT is 100% safe if you take the ♠A, cash the ♣K and run the ♣J into the North hand. If the club finesse wins, you have ten tricks while if it loses, nine tricks are guaranteed on any return by North (and ten tricks if North continues spades).

43. You, West, hold:

```
♠ A 4 3          Dealer West : North-South vulnerable
♡ A K            WEST     NORTH    EAST     SOUTH
◇ J 9 6 3        ?
♣ A K 7 3
```

What is your opening bid?

Answer: The standard approach is to open 1♣ and make a strong rebid in no-trumps. Some would open 1◇, the weaker four-card suit, in the hope that if the contract ends in no-trumps, the opponents will shy away from diamonds since this is a suit that you have bid. The stronger your hand, the more reasonable is this approach as you are likely to win the bidding. With only 15-16 points, it is better to open in the stronger suit for that is what you want partner to lead if the opponents buy the contract.

```
♠ A 4 3          Dealer West : North-South vulnerable
♡ A K            WEST     NORTH    EAST     SOUTH
◇ J 9 6 3        1◇       No       1♠       No
♣ A K 7 3        ?
```

What do you do now?

Answer: This is one of the problems caused by the jump to 3NT to show 19 points. If partner has five spades, 4♠ may be best but if you jump to 3NT, partner cannot safely explore the possibility of a 5-3 fit.

Playing the structure suggested in Problems #41 and #42, West would jump to 2NT, showing 19-20 points and forcing to game. Now East can bid 3♠ to show a five-card suit and elicit three-card support.

```
♠ A 4 3                            ♠ K J 8 2
♡ A K              N               ♡ 5 3 2
◇ J 9 6 3      W       E           ◇ 10 2
♣ A K 7 3                          ♣ Q 10 5 2
                   S
```

Against 3NT, North leads the ♡4. How do you plan the play?

```
              ♠ 10 9 6 5
              ♡ Q 10 8 4
              ◇ K
              ♣ J 9 8 6
♠ A 4 3                        ♠ K J 8 2
♡ A K                          ♡ 5 3 2
◇ J 9 6 3                      ◇ 10 2
♣ A K 7 3                      ♣ Q 10 5 2
              ♠ Q 7
              ♡ J 9 7 6
              ◇ A Q 8 7 5 4
              ♣ 4
```

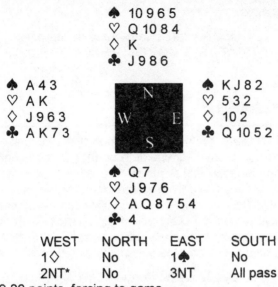

WEST	NORTH	EAST	SOUTH
1◇	No	1♠	No
2NT*	No	3NT	All pass

*19-20 points, forcing to game

There are seven instant winners. The clubs are likely to provide an eighth and the ninth can come from the spades, either with the ♠Q onside or thanks to a 3-3 break.

At trick two, tackle the clubs. Playing the winners *opposite* the tenace first, you start with the ♣A and ♣K. This precaution proves vital when North turns up with ♣J-x-x-x. If you play the ♣Q on the first or second round of clubs, you have a club loser.

With four tricks available in clubs, you need only three tricks from the spades. As the hearts and diamonds are stopped, you can afford a loser in spades if this improves your chances of three spade tricks. Finesse the ♣10 but leave the ♣Q as an entry to dummy. Now cash the ♠K and play a spade to your ace. This guards against ♠Q doubleton with South. When the ♠Q drops you are home. If North had started with the ♠Q you would still be all right by leading a spade towards dummy's ♠J-8.

If a bad club break meant that you had only three club tricks, you would need to play for four spade tricks by cashing the ♠A and finessing the ♠J next. If North holds ♠Q-x-x, you would succeed. Note how the play in spades varies according to how many spade tricks are needed.

44. You, East, hold:

♠ A 10
♡ A 2
♢ A Q 10 9 2
♣ K Q 7 2

Dealer North : East-West vulnerable

WEST	NORTH	EAST	SOUTH
	1♡	?	

What should East do?

Answer: East is too strong for a simple overcall in diamonds or for a 1NT overcall (16-18 HCP), even if you ignore the off-shape. The best start is Double. The main risk is a reply in spades but over 1♠ or 2♠ you can bid no-trumps or show the diamonds.

You are most unlikely to hear a reply of 4♠. Since North opened the bidding and you have 19 HCP, West is most unlikely to have the strength to justify a jump to 4♠. If partner does bid 4♠, partner will have considerable length in spades and about seven losers. You would then try for 6♠.

♠ A 10
♡ A 2
♢ A Q 10 9 2
♣ K Q 7 2

Dealer North : East-West vulnerable

WEST	NORTH	EAST	SOUTH
	1♡	Double	No
2♠	No	?	

What now?

Answer: West's 2♠ shows around 10-12 points (including shortage points) but does not promise any more than four spades. You can expect a hand of 7-8 losers. 3♢ would be sensible (a change of suit is forcing after a jump reply to a takeout double) but 3NT also has merit. If partner has a fit for diamonds, that will be useful for no-trumps and if partner does not have values in diamonds, you do not want to be in 5♢.

♠ K Q 7 6 5 3
♡ 10 9 4
♢ J 7 5
♣ 6

♠ A 10
♡ A 2
♢ A Q 10 9 2
♣ K Q 7 2

Against 4♠, North leads the ♡K. Plan West's play.

```
                        ♠ 4
                        ♡ K Q 7 5
                        ◇ K 8 6 3
                        ♣ A J 8 4

    ♠ K Q 7 6 5 3                       ♠ A 10
    ♡ 10 9 4                            ♡ A 2
    ◇ J 7 5          W      E           ◇ A Q 10 9 2
    ♣ 6                                 ♣ K Q 7 2

                        ♠ J 9 8 2
                        ♡ J 8 6 3
                        ◇ 4
                        ♣ 10 9 5 3
```

WEST	NORTH	EAST	SOUTH
	1♡	Double	No
2♠	No	3NT	No
4♠	No	No	No

The king of diamonds is likely to be with North but if not, there is some danger of losing two hearts, a club and a diamond. Likewise, trumps are probably 3-2, but if not, you might lose a spade, two hearts and a club.

If everything were rosy, you might make twelve tricks by drawing trumps followed by five diamond tricks. As your task is not twelve tricks but just ten, it pays to take some precautions.

When this deal arose, Lord Lever was declarer. He took the ♡A at trick one and played the ♣K next. This set up a club trick for a heart discard, if necessary, while dummy still had trumps to take care of heart plays by the opponents. North won with the ♣A, cashed the ♡Q and played a third heart. Declarer ruffed with the ♠10, cashed the ♠A, ruffed a club and drew two more rounds of trumps. When they failed to break, he simply took the diamond finesse and made the contract.

See what happens if declarer plays ♠A and another spade at tricks two and three. If West cashes a third spade and then leads the ◇J, South can ruff in on the diamonds and the defence comes to one spade, two hearts and a club.

45. You, West, hold:

♠ A 8 3   Dealer West : Both vulnerable
♡ A K J 9 4   WEST   NORTH   EAST   SOUTH
♢ K 6 3   ?
♣ A Q

What would you choose as your opening bid?

Answer: If available, you could start with a Benjamin 2♣ (intending to rebid 2♡ after a 2♢ reply), but an Acol 2♡ becomes awkward after partner's 2NT reply. The practical bid is 2NT. This is definitely best if you are using a 3♣ response as 5-card major Stayman, but even without that, 2NT is likely to lead to the best spot. A lot of the time you will finish in 3NT and your minor suit holdings make it attractive for you to be the declarer in no-trumps.

	WEST	NORTH	EAST	SOUTH
♠ A 8 3	2NT	No	3♣	No
♡ A K J 9 4	3♡	No	5♡	No
♢ K 6 3	?			
♣ A Q				

3♣ was 5-card major Stayman and 3♡ showed five hearts. What do you do now?

Answer: Partner's jump to 5♡ invites a slam and asks you to focus on the quality of your hearts. You can expect partner to hold the values for slam but to have weak hearts. As you have excellent hearts and a strong all-round hand, bid 6♡.

♠ A 8 3		♠ 9 6 4
♡ A K J 9 4	N	♡ Q 5 3
♢ K 6 3	W E	♢ A 7 5 4
♣ A Q	S	♣ K J 10

Against 6♡, North leads the ♠K. East's heart holding is stronger than expected but dummy is a disappointment. With no ruffing value, 4♡ by East would have been enough. Still, you cannot worry about that now. Plan your play to make 6♡.

```
                    ♠ K Q J 10
                    ♡ 7 2
                    ◇ Q 10 2
                    ♣ 9 8 5 3

♠ A 8 3                                    ♠ 9 6 4
♡ A K J 9 4        N                       ♡ Q 5 3
◇ K 6 3         W     E                     ◇ A 7 5 4
♣ A Q              S                        ♣ K J 10

                    ♠ 7 5 2
                    ♡ 10 8 6
                    ◇ J 9 8
                    ♣ 7 6 4 2
```

WEST	NORTH	EAST	SOUTH
2NT	No	3♣	No
3♡	No	5♡	No
6♡	No	No	No

The slam would be excellent if East's pattern were 2-3-4-4 with the same high cards but be grateful it is not 4-3-4-2 when it would be hopeless. While the slam will fail most of the time, at least there is some chance.

You have two spade losers and a diamond loser. One of these can be discarded on the third round of clubs but that still leaves two losers. You start with eleven tricks (barring an outlandish trump break) and the only hope for a twelfth trick is from a 3-3 break in diamonds.

Obviously you cannot afford to concede a diamond trick as that exposes you to two spade losers. As there is only one hope, play for the trumps to be 3-2 and the diamonds 3-3.

Take the ♠A, cash the ♡A and the ♡K, leaving the ♡Q as an entry to dummy. Continue with ♣A, ♣Q overtaken by the king, and ♣J to discard a diamond. Then play a diamond to the king, diamond to the ace, ruff the third diamond high, cross to the ♡Q, drawing the last trump, and cash the thirteenth diamond on which a spade loser is discarded. Sit back and glow if you will, but do not expect any congratulations from the opponents.

46. You, West, hold:

♠	A K Q 9 2	Dealer West : East-West vulnerable			
♡	K 8	WEST	NORTH	EAST	SOUTH
◇	9 5 3	1♠	No	4◇	No
♣	K 7 4	?			

4 ◇ is a splinter. What does that mean?

Answer: Splinter bids are used to show a hand with high cards worth game at least plus support for partner's suit and a singleton or void in the suit bid. You can expect East to hold four or more spades, 11+ HCP and one or no diamonds.

What is the purpose of the splinter?

Answer: A splinter invites slam. With a good holding in the short suit or with considerable extra strength, partner should head towards slam. With minimum values and wasted strength in the short suit, partner should sign off in game.

What are the bad holdings opposite the short suit?

Answer: The king, queen and jack lose their value opposite the shortage. A singleton opposite a singleton is of no extra benefit and a doubleton opposite the singleton is also poor, as you can score only one ruff.

The good holdings are x-x-x, x-x-x-x, A-x-x or A-x-x-x.

What action do you take after 4 ◇?

Answer: With a good holding in diamonds and some extra strength, you should head for slam. Bid 4NT asking for key cards. Opposite one key card, sign off in 5♠; opposite two, bid 6♠ and opposite three, explore grand slam possibilities.

♠ A K Q 9 2		♠ 8 7 5 4
♡ K 8		♡ A 10 9 7 6
◇ 9 5 3		◇ 6
♣ K 7 4		♣ A Q 8

Against 6♠, North leads ♣J, South playing ♣2. Plan the play.

```
              ♠ J
              ♡ J 4
              ◇ 10 8 4 2
              ♣ J 10 9 6 5 3
♠ A K Q 9 2                        ♠ 8 7 5 4
♡ K 8            N                 ♡ A 10 9 7 6
◇ 9 5 3      W       E             ◇ 6
♣ K 7 4          S                 ♣ A Q 8
              ♠ 10 6 3
              ♡ Q 5 3 2
              ◇ A K Q J 7
              ♣ 2
```

Bob Hamman, ranked #1 in the world, won the first trick in hand, drew trumps, cashed ♡K, crossed to ♡A and ruffed a heart. With hearts 4-2, he was home. A club to dummy was followed by a heart ruff, a club to dummy and the last heart, on which he pitched a diamond. Another diamond was later ruffed in dummy.

It would be reasonable to win the lead and play a diamond next, planning to ruff two diamonds in dummy. As the cards lie, the defence could then defeat the slam by North winning the diamond and giving South a club ruff. Hamman reasoned that if trumps were 2-2, the diamond losers could be ruffed but otherwise it was safer to draw trumps and hope to set up the fifth heart.

South might have suggested a sacrifice in diamonds. Repeated trump leads do maximum damage to a diamond contract but if North had five diamonds, the sacrifice might be quite cheap.

Doubling 4◇ to ask for a diamond lead has no merit, as there is little point in leading dummy's singleton. Some double a splinter to indicate a long suit for a sacrifice, others double to ask for a specific lead outside trumps and the splinter suit (such as the higher-ranking outside suit). If you play the latter, you would need to bid 5◇ on the South cards to institute a sacrifice auction. As North is marked with short spades on the bidding, North is likely to have a few diamonds and at the vulnerability, 5◇ doubled is unlikely to cost too much.

47. You, East, hold:

♠ Q J 6   Dealer West : East-West vulnerable
♡ - - -   WEST   NORTH   EAST   SOUTH
♢ A K 6 4 3   1♠   No   ?
♣ A Q 6 5 2

What should East respond?

Answer: Even if playing five-card majors, it is premature to support spades. Do not consider a 4♡ splinter (see #46). You should have a minimum of four trumps for a splinter. With a strong two-suited hand, a jump shift is not recommended. Simply change suit with 2♢ (higher-ranking first with a 5-5).

♠ Q J 6   Dealer West : East-West vulnerable
♡ - - -   WEST   NORTH   EAST   SOUTH
♢ A K 6 4 3   1♠   No   2♢   No
♣ A Q 6 5 2   2♠   No   ?

What should East do now?

Answer: 6♠ looks a good bet but 7♠ could be there opposite as little as ♠A-K-x-x-x-x and the ♣K. Bid 3♣ to explore further.

♠ Q J 6   WEST   NORTH   EAST   SOUTH
♡ - - -   1♠   No   2♢   No
♢ A K 6 4 3   2♠   No   3♣   No
♣ A Q 6 5 2   3NT   No   ?

And now?

Answer: As partner has a minimum with some wasted values in hearts, the grand slam is no longer likely. Settle for 6♠.

♠ K 10 9 8 4 3   ♠ Q J 6
♡ K Q J   ♡ - - -
♢ 10 5   ♢ A K 6 4 3
♣ K 10   ♣ A Q 6 5 2

Against 6♠, North leads ♠A, then ♠2, South following both times. How would you continue as declarer?

101

♠ A 2
♥ 10 8 4 2
♦ Q 2
♣ J 9 7 4 3

♠ K 10 9 8 4 3　　♠ Q J 6
♥ K Q J 　　　　　　♥ - - -
♦ 10 5 　　　　　　 ♦ A K 6 4 3
♣ K 10 　　　　　　 ♣ A Q 6 5 2

♠ 7 5
♥ A 9 7 6 5 3
♦ J 9 8 7
♣ 8

WEST	NORTH	EAST	SOUTH
1♠	No	2♦	No
2♣	No	3♣	No
3NT	No	6♣	All pass

After ♠A and another spade, dummy has only one trump left. You can ruff one heart and discard a heart on the third round of clubs but what about your third heart?

The ruffing finesse play is only a 50% chance and you can do much better than that. If either minor suit breaks 3-3 or 4-2, you can set up at least one additional trick there to take care of your third heart.

Which suit should you tackle first? Clubs seem the instinctive move as they are stronger, but correct technique is to try the diamonds first. If the clubs are 3-3, they can wait. If they are 4-2, you can set up the fifth club with just one ruff and the entry to dummy will be the heart ruff.

To set up the diamonds if they are 4-2 requires two ruffs and two entries to dummy. If you have played off the clubs first, you no longer have two entries to dummy. On the actual deal you fail if you try the clubs first. Check it out.

So, cash ♦A, ♦K, ruff a diamond, play three rounds of clubs, pitching a heart, and ruff the fourth diamond. Ruff a heart in dummy and discard your last heart on dummy's diamond winner.

48. You, West, hold:

♠ A 4   Dealer West : Nil vulnerable
♡ A K 9 5 2   WEST   NORTH   EAST   SOUTH
♢ A K 9 4   1♡   No   1NT   No
♣ 7 3   ?

What should West do now?

Answer: You have 'only' 18 HCP but what a superb 18. Aces are generally undervalued in the standard point count. They are worth closer to 4¼ points relative to the other honours. That is why you add a point when holding all four aces.

Jacks are slightly over-valued, particularly unsupported jacks. A hand in which the HCP are made up of only aces and kings and no jacks is worth upgrading.

Here you should insist on game but to bid 3NT is misguided. The clubs might be wide open but that is not the main reason. As partner will not hold four spades or four hearts, chances are that partner does have at least four clubs. More importantly, the right contract might be in hearts. 4♡ or 4♠ with an eight-card or better major fit will generally succeed more often than 3NT. Accordingly, you should not settle for 3NT until you have determined that no eight-card major fit exists.

Here your best move is to jump to 3♢. The jump-shift insists on game and by rebidding in a lower suit, you confirm that you hold at least five cards in the suit opened. Now partner's first duty will be to support hearts with three trumps.

3NT is likely to be superior to a 5-3 major fit when you hold a 5-3-3-2 pattern opposite a 4-3-3-3, particularly if the doubleton is opposite the four-card suit. This is not easy to diagnose for natural bidders. Also, when you hold around 30-32 points, you are likely to make as many tricks in no-trumps as in your major.

♠ A 4   ♠ 9 6 5
♡ A K 9 5 2   N   ♡ 8 4 3
♢ A K 9 4   W   E   ♢ 10 6 3
♣ 7 3   S   ♣ A Q 8 4

Against 4♡, North leads the ♣2. Plan the play. Be specific.

```
                    ♠ K 10 8 3
                    ♡ 10
                    ◇ Q 8 7 5
                    ♣ K 9 6 2
    ♠ A 4                            ♠ 9 6 5
    ♡ A K 9 5 2        N             ♡ 8 4 3
    ◇ A K 9 4     W         E        ◇ 10 6 3
    ♣ 7 3              S             ♣ A Q 8 4
                    ♠ Q J 7 2
                    ♡ Q J 7 6
                    ◇ J 2
                    ♣ J 10 5
```

WEST	NORTH	EAST	SOUTH
1♡	No	1NT	No
3◇	No	4♡	All pass

After the game-forcing jump to 3◇, 4♡ is weaker than 3♡.

4♡ is anything but secure. Not only is there a possible loser in each suit but you also need to deal with your fourth diamond and may have to cater for a 4-1 trump break.

Since you cannot discard a club and cannot afford to lose a club, you need all the luck you can find. Try the ♣Q. When that holds, play a trump to your ace. When an honour drops from North, consider a bad trump break. Players rarely part with honours willingly and so an honour dropping may well be a singleton.

To cater for four trumps with South, play a club to dummy's ace and lead a second trump. If South plays low, insert the 9. If North can win that, only one trump is missing. You can draw that later.

When the ♡9 wins, test the diamonds with ◇A, ◇K. After the ◇J drops from South, cash ♡K and lead the ◇4. North wins but the ◇9 is high. You lose one spade, one heart and one diamond.

If South plays a heart honour at trick four, you win with the ♡K and cash ◇A, ◇K. Whether or not a diamond honour drops, you play a third diamond. If North wins, North cannot play another trump. You can later ruff a diamond in dummy and whether or not South over-ruffs, you are all right.

49. You, West, hold:

♠ 7 4	Dealer West : Nil vulnerable			
♡ A K J	WEST	NORTH	EAST	SOUTH
◇ A K 7 5 3	?			
♣ K Q J				

What would you open with the West cards?

Answer: The weakness in spades is a nuisance but there is no better start than 2NT. To open 1◇ risks partner passing and a missed game. To open with an Acol 2◇ is not appealing either. What would you do after a 2NT reply?

It is usually best to open 2NT with a 5-3-3-2 pattern and 20-22 points. If one of the suits is unguarded, so be it. Take your chances. With the same pattern and 23+ points, open 2♣ and rebid no-trumps if the five-card suit is a minor and rebid in the major if that is your five-card suit.

♠ 7 4	WEST	NORTH	EAST	SOUTH
♡ A K J	2NT	No	3♠	No
◇ A K 7 5 3	3NT	No	4NT	No
♣ K Q J	?			

3♠ was natural, showing a five-card suit and 3NT denied spade support. What do you now?

Answer: 4NT in auctions such as this is usually played as inviting partner to bid slam if better than minimum. Your lack of any high card in spades is a drawback but against that, you have 21 HCP and a respectable five-card suit yourself. Faint heart ne'er won fair contract. Bid 6NT.

♠ 7 4		♠ A K 6 3 2
♡ A K J		♡ Q 4 2
◇ A K 7 5 3		◇ Q 10
♣ K Q J		♣ 10 9 8

Against 6NT, North leads the queen of spades. Plan the play.

```
                    ♠ Q J 10
                    ♡ 9 7 5 3
                    ◇ J 6
                    ♣ A 7 5 4
♠ 7 4                                    ♠ A K 6 3 2
♡ A K J                                  ♡ Q 4 2
◇ A K 7 5 3         N                    ◇ Q 10
♣ K Q J          W     E                 ♣ 10 9 8
                    S
                    ♠ 9 8 5
                    ♡ 10 8 6
                    ◇ 9 8 4 2
                    ♣ 6 3 2
```

WEST	NORTH	EAST	SOUTH
2NT	No	3♠	No
3NT	No	4NT	No
6NT	No	No	No

You have to lose a trick in clubs to create two winners there. Even then, you have only ten tricks and as you cannot afford to lose another trick, you must play the diamonds for five tricks.

The question then arises, what is the best play to try to garner five diamond tricks. There are two possibilities: cash the queen, king and ace of diamonds and hope that they split 3-3. That is just below a 36%.

The alternative is play a low diamond from hand and finesse dummy's ten of diamonds. That will produce five tricks if North began with J-x, J-x-x or J-x-x-x in diamonds. That is a 50% chance of the 4-2 breaks and the 3-3 breaks. The 4-2 split occurs about 48% of the time. Half of that is 24% and half of the 3-3s is 18%. That totals 42%, quite a bit better than the 36% of just the 3-3 break. 6% may not seem much but ask your bank manager for 6% more interest on your moneys deposited with the bank and see what reaction that produces.

Take the ♠A and knock out the ♣A. Win the spade exit, cross to the ♡A and play a diamond to the ten. When that wins, cash the ◇Q and claim twelve tricks when both opponents follow.

50. You, West, hold:

♠ 10 2	Dealer West : Both vulnerable			
♡ 2	WEST	NORTH	EAST	SOUTH
◇ A K Q J 4	1◇	No	1♠	No
♣ A Q 5 4 3	?			

What should West bid now?

Answer: You have a strong two-suiter but not enough for a jump-shift to 3♣. Give partner six or seven points scattered in the majors and you have little hope for 3NT and even less in a minor suit game. It is enough to bid 2♣. If partner cannot muster another bid after that, game is wildly unlikely.

♠ 10 2	WEST	NORTH	EAST	SOUTH
♡ 2	1◇	No	1♠	No
◇ A K Q J 4	2♣	No	2♠	No
♣ A Q 5 4 3	?			

What now?

Answer: Partner's 2♠ should be a weak hand (6-9 points) with a six-card or longer suit, or a strong five-carder with at least three honours. You are definitely worth an effort and the best chance for game lies in spades. Your singleton heart should protect partner against quick losers there and the solid diamonds should allow partner to discard some losers.

Do not bid 3♣. That would imply no tolerance for spades. Invite game with 3♠, or if you have a macho personality, bid 4♠.

♠ Q J 9 8 4 3		♠ 10 2
♡ A 9 8 7	N	♡ 2
◇ 3 2	W E	◇ A K Q J 4
♣ 6	S	♣ A Q 5 4 3

Note that East and West have been transposed. Excuse our little deception but had the question been posed with you as East, you might reasonably deduce that you would not become the declarer.

Against 4♠, North leads the king of spades and switches to the king of hearts. How would you plan the play?

```
              ♠ A K 5
              ♡ K Q J 4
              ◇ 10 5
              ♣ 9 8 7 2
♠ Q J 9 8 4 3                    ♠ 10 2
♡ A 9 8 7          N             ♡ 2
◇ 3 2          W       E         ◇ A K Q J 4
♣ 6                S            ♣ A Q 5 4 3
              ♠ 7 6
              ♡ 10 6 5 3
              ◇ 9 8 7 6
              ♣ K J 10
```

WEST	NORTH	EAST	SOUTH
		1◇	No
1♠	No	2♣	No
2♠	No	3♠	No
4♠	No	No	No

The danger is clear. After taking the ace of hearts, you have three potential losers in hearts. You could ruff a heart and start on the diamonds. If they break 3-3, one of your heart losers goes on the third diamond. When you play a fourth diamond and discard your last heart, an opponent will ruff but you lose just three trump tricks.

That line requires diamonds to be 3-3, only about a 36% chance. As the club finesse is 50%, a better line would be to finesse the ♣Q at trick 3. If this wins, discard a diamond on the ♣A, ruff a club, ruff a heart and run the diamonds, discarding a heart on the third round. If you chose this approach, good, but no cigar. You can do even better.

As you have only two top trump losers, you can afford to lose another trick. Therefore, why not let North have the heart trick? That is precisely what the late Terence Reese, one of the world's greatest players, did. Dummy would take care of the next heart and declarer can deal with any move the defence makes. If North removes dummy's trump, declarer still has control of the hearts and can use dummy's diamond to discard heart losers.

51. You, East, hold:

```
♠ A Q J          Dealer West : Both vulnerable
♡ A K 7 5 4      WEST    NORTH    EAST    SOUTH
◇ A 3            1◇      No       ?
♣ 9 7 3
```

What should East respond?

Answer: There is no need to jump-shift. If the hearts were more powerful (such as A-K-J-10-x) we would favour 2♡ but with no such depth, 1♡ is preferred. West's natural and unforced rebid may allow you to judge his strength better.

```
♠ A Q J          Dealer West : Both vulnerable
♡ A K 7 5 4      WEST    NORTH    EAST    SOUTH
◇ A 3            1◇      No       1♡      No
♣ 9 7 3          2◇      No       ?
```

What next?

Answer: 3NT would be cavalier with nothing in clubs. Best is 2♠, new suit and therefore forcing. Partner will not raise spades as the 2◇ rebid denied four spades.

```
♠ A Q J          WEST    NORTH    EAST    SOUTH
♡ A K 7 5 4      1◇      No       1♡      No
◇ A 3            2◇      No       2♠      No
♣ 9 7 3          3NT     No       ?
```

And now?

Answer: West has the clubs stopped and is at the top end of a minimum opening. Had West rebid 2NT, 3NT would have been enough. After the jump to 3NT, you are worth a shot at 6NT.

```
♠ K 5 2                          ♠ A Q J
♡ 6 2                            ♡ A K 7 5 4
◇ K 10 8 7 4 2                   ◇ A 3
♣ A K                            ♣ 9 7 3
```

Against 6NT, North leads the ♠8. Plan the play.

```
                    ♠ 8 7 4
                    ♡ J 8
                    ◇ Q J 6 5
                    ♣ J 8 6 4

♠ K 5 2                                 ♠ A Q J
♡ 6 2                  N                ♡ A K 7 5 4
◇ K 10 8 7 4 2     W       E           ◇ A 3
♣ A K                  S               ♣ 9 7 3

                    ♠ 10 9 6 3
                    ♡ Q 10 9 3
                    ◇ 9
                    ♣ Q 10 5 2
```

WEST	NORTH	EAST	SOUTH
1◇	No	1♡	No
2◇	No	2♠	No
3NT	No	6NT	All pass

You have nine tricks on top and only the diamonds can provide the extra three needed. There will be no problem if the diamonds are 3-2. Can you guard against any of the 4-1 splits?

If South has ◇Q-J-9-x, you can do nothing. After a diamond to the ace and a diamond back, South inserts an honour and you must lose two diamond tricks. However, if North started with bare ◇Q, ◇J or ◇9, you can deal with this quite comfortably.

What if North started with four diamonds? You are doomed if North began with Q-9-x-x or J-9-x-x but you can deal with singleton 9 with South by leading the ◇10 from hand.

Indeed, strange as it may seem, leading the ten of diamonds caters for every 4-1 break against which it is possible to guard. Suppose you lead the ten and North began with bare queen, jack or nine. Win with dummy's ace, return a diamond, and cover South's card as cheaply as possible. South cannot score more than one trick. In addition the ◇10 pins the singleton ◇9 with South, as in the layout above. If North plays low, run the ten. If North covers you win with dummy's ace and lose just one trick.

This combination is unlikely to occur often but carry the deal with you. It makes sparkling entertainment at a cocktail party.

52. You, West, hold:

♠ Q 10 7 2   Dealer North : East-West vulnerable
♡ Q 9 3   WEST   NORTH   EAST   SOUTH
♢ K Q   1♠   Double   No
♣ Q 10 8 6   ?

What action should West take?

Answer: When replying to a takeout double, you first decide what you will bid and then how high to bid it. The order of priority is unbid major first, no-trumps second, minor suit last. One qualification is that the expectancy for 1NT is 6-9 points. With 0-5 points, choose a suit reply. Also, any no-trump reply should include at least one stopper in their suit.

Here your choices would be clubs or no-trumps. Using the above priorities, you should be bidding no-trumps. 2NT (10-12 points) is the appropriate level. For 3NT, 13+ points are expected.

Do not consider passing for penalties. To leave a takeout double in at the one-level, your trumps should be stronger than declarer's. The absolute minimum is five trumps including three honours. Even that may not be enough to inflict serious damage. Here your trumps are too short and too weak. In addition, at this vulnerability you should be striving for game rather than borderline chances for penalties.

Suppose East rebids 3♡ over 2NT. What now?

Answer: To bid 3♡, East will hold five hearts. As 2NT denied four hearts, according to the priority list, partner would not introduce a four-card heart suit. You should raise to 4♡, as the 5-3 fit is likely to play better than 3NT, especially as partner is likely to hold a singleton or a void in spades.

♠ Q 10 7 2   ♠ K 3
♡ Q 9 3   ♡ K J 10 8
♢ K Q   ♢ A 4 2
♣ Q 10 8 6   ♣ K J 9 5

Against 3NT, North leads the ♣6. How do you plan the play?

111

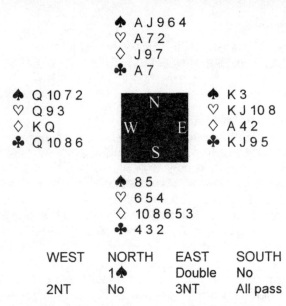

```
            ♠ A J 9 6 4
            ♡ A 7 2
            ◇ J 9 7
            ♣ A 7

♠ Q 10 7 2              ♠ K 3
♡ Q 9 3                 ♡ K J 10 8
◇ K Q                   ◇ A 4 2
♣ Q 10 8 6              ♣ K J 9 5

            ♠ 8 5
            ♡ 6 5 4
            ◇ 10 8 6 5 3
            ♣ 4 3 2
```

WEST	NORTH	EAST	SOUTH
	1♠	Double	No
2NT	No	3NT	All pass

You have three winners on top in diamonds. You can set up three tricks in clubs and three in hearts to make the contract, plus some extras in spades. The only problem is that to set up these winners you will have to lose the lead twice, obviously to North who must have almost every missing point.

The instinctive move is to play low from dummy at trick one and let the lead come to your tenace. The Rule of 11 tells you that South has only one spade higher than the ♠6. 11 minus 6 (the value of the card led) = 5 (which is the number of cards higher than the card led in the other three hands). You can see four cards higher than the 6. The other one is with South.

You can already visualise the play. You win trick one with, say, the ♠10 and lead a club. North wins, captures the ♠K with the ace and leads a high spade to knock out your last stopper. When you play a heart, North wins and cashes spades. North wins two aces and may have enough spade tricks to beat you before you can establish the tricks you need.

You have a satisfying counter. Play dummy's ♠K at trick one. This is bound to win and when North regains the lead, North cannot set up the spades without giving you three tricks there.

53. You, West, hold:

♠ A 8   Dealer West : Nil vulnerable
♡ K J 8 6   WEST   NORTH   EAST   SOUTH
◇ A 10 9 6 5   ?
♣ 3 2

What would you do as dealer?

Answer: It is not recommended to open 1NT with a 5-4-2-2 but if you do, most of the strength should be in the doubletons. Here, with most of your strength in your long suits, open 1◇.

♠ A 8   Dealer West : Nil vulnerable
♡ K J 8 6   WEST   NORTH   EAST   SOUTH
◇ A 10 9 6 5   1◇   No   2♣   No
♣ 3 2   ?

What now?

Answer: You are not strong enough to bid 2♡. A 'reverse', changing suit beyond two of the suit opened, shows a strong hand, usually 16 points or more. Rebid 2◇.

♠ A 8   WEST   NORTH   EAST   SOUTH
♡ K J 8 6   1◇   No   2♣   No
◇ A 10 9 6 5   2◇   No   2♠   No
♣ 3 2   ?

What now?

Answer: With the hearts stopped, you should rebid 2NT. There is not enough for 3NT. Partner will know your hand is not balanced. You did not open 1NT but 2◇ showed a minimum opening.

♠ A 8   ♠ K Q 9 2
♡ K J 8 6   ♡ 7 3
◇ A 10 9 6 5   ◇ 8 2
♣ 3 2   ♣ A Q J 10 5

Against 3NT, North leads the ♡4, taken by South with the ace. Back comes the ♡9. How do you plan the play from here?

113

```
               ♠ 10 5 3
               ♡ Q 10 5 4 2
               ◇ Q J 3
               ♣ 7 6
♠ A 8                              ♠ K Q 9 2
♡ K J 8 6                          ♡ 7 3
◇ A 10 9 6 5        N              ◇ 8 2
♣ 3 2          W         E         ♣ A Q J 10 5
                    S
               ♠ J 7 6 4
               ♡ A 9
               ◇ K 7 4
               ♣ K 9 8 4
```

WEST	NORTH	EAST	SOUTH
1◇	No	2♣	No
2◇	No	2♠	No
2NT	No	3NT	All pass

After the heart lead to South and a heart return, you have six top tricks. The obvious place for the extra tricks is the club suit.

Could anything go wrong if you finesse the ♡J? If it loses and a heart is returned you score an extra heart trick. You are not concerned with overtricks, only with giving yourself the best chance to make 3NT. If the ♡J loses, North might recognise that with such strong black suits in dummy, a shift to diamonds is the only hope, despite your having bid them twice. You could then lose two hearts, two diamonds and a club.

At Lederer's Club, kibitzers were given a small bell and if they spotted an error by the player they were watching, they would ring the bell. If their analysis was correct, they would replace that player in the game. As a young man, Claude Rodrigue, yet to become a European Champion, was declarer on this deal. His kibitzer was unable to bell him as Claude rose with the ♡K at trick two and then finessed in clubs. South won but had no heart to return. If he had, the suit would be 4-3 and declarer would lose only three hearts and a club.

Did you play the ♡J at trick two? Ding, ding, ding, ding, ding.

54. You, West, hold:

♠ K 8 5 3	Dealer West : East-West vulnerable			
♡ K Q 9 8 3	WEST	NORTH	EAST	SOUTH
◇ 6	No	1◇	1NT	No
♣ 6 4 2	?			

What action do you take?

Answer: You have enough to try for a game but the right spot could be in hearts, spades or no-trumps. To cater for all possibilities, your best move is 2♣ Stayman. If partner bids 2♡ or 2♠, raise to game.

Some play that bidding the enemy suit replaces Stayman. In that case you would bid 2◇.

If you use transfers and play the same methods over the 1NT overcall as over a 1NT opening, a sensible strategy, then you could bid 2◇ as a transfer to hearts and show the spades next.

♠ K 8 5 3	WEST	NORTH	EAST	SOUTH
♡ K Q 9 8 3	No	1◇	1NT	No
◇ 6	2♣	No	2◇	No
♣ 6 4 2	?			

What now?

Answer: As partner has no major, there is no 4-4 spade fit, but a 5-3 fit in hearts is possible. Do not settle for no-trumps until you are satisfied that no major suit fit exists. Jump to 3♡ showing five hearts and forcing to game. That may seem a little pushy with only 8 HCP but with East's strong hand sitting over North, the cards should be well placed for your side.

♠ K 8 5 3		♠ 6 2
♡ K Q 9 8 3	N	♡ A J 10
◇ 6	W E	◇ A 7 5 2
♣ 6 4 2	S	♣ A K J 3

East raises 3♡ to 4♡ and all pass. North leads the king of diamonds. How would you plan the play?

```
                    ♠ A Q 9 4
                    ♡ 7 6
                    ◇ K Q J 10 3
                    ♣ 8 5
  ♠ K 8 5 3                           ♠ 6 2
  ♡ K Q 9 8 3                         ♡ A J 10
  ◇ 6              ◇ A 7 5 2
  ♣ 6 4 2                             ♣ A K J 3
                    ♠ J 10 7
                    ♡ 5 4 2
                    ◇ 9 8 4
                    ♣ Q 10 9 7
```

WEST	NORTH	EAST	SOUTH
No	1◇	1NT	No
2♣	No	2◇	No
3♡	No	4♡	All pass

Five hearts, one diamond and two clubs make eight tricks. A sound plan is to win the ◇A and play a low spade from both hands. As North almost certainly has ♠A, playing your ♠K will not gain. Even if they shift to trumps, you can ruff the third spade in dummy. If North has fewer than four spades and the ♠A has fallen, the ♠K and one ruff in dummy give you two extra tricks.

If the ♠A fails to drop in three rounds, you can still finesse the jack of clubs. As North opened the bidding and only 15 HCP are missing, North is highly likely to hold the ♣Q.

As good as this plan is, there is a better one. When dummy's trumps are so strong, ruffing losers with the long trump hand can produce extra tricks if you can ruff often enough to shorten the long trump hand below the length of the trumps opposite. Ruffing three diamonds in your hand creates one extra trick and a club ruff in hand will produce another.

Take the ◇A, ruff a diamond, cross to ♣A, ruff a diamond, cross to ♣K, ruff a diamond and concede a club. On regaining the lead you can organise to ruff dummy's last club. Your tricks are ◇A, ♣A-K, four ruffs in hand and dummy's three hearts.

55. You, East, hold:

♠ K 6	Dealer East : East-West vulnerable			
♡ A K Q	WEST	NORTH	EAST	SOUTH
◇ A K Q J 10			2♣	No
♣ A 9 2	2◇	No	?	

What is your rebid?

Answer: You are too strong for 2NT and the contenders are 3◇ or 3NT. After partner's negative, slam is unlikely as you have three losers. 5◇ is no sure thing but 3NT is a certainty even opposite a Yarborough, as long as you are declarer.

♠ K 6	WEST	NORTH	EAST	SOUTH
♡ A K Q			2♣	No
◇ A K Q J 10	2◇	No	3NT	No
♣ A 9 2	4NT	No	?	

What now?

Answer: 4NT is not asking for aces but inviting you to bid slam if you have more than just a minimum for your 3NT rebid. On the downside you have three losers and partner cannot be expected to provide three high card winners. Few would criticise a pass of 4NT.

On the other hand, it is possible for partner to have ♠Q-J-x and the ♣K, or even just ♠A-Q-x, although with 1½ quick tricks that is on the borderline of a positive response.

If you intend to bid on, 6NT is reasonable but you could also jump to 6◇. If partner cannot support diamonds or has no ruffing value, partner can always revert to 6NT.

♠ Q 3 2		♠ K 6
♡ 6 4	N	♡ A K Q
◇ 7 5 3	W E	◇ A K Q J 10
♣ K 8 6 5 4	S	♣ A 9 2

You, West, are declarer in 6◇, thanks to your 2◇ response. North leads the ten of hearts. How would you plan the play?

```
                  ♠ A 8 7 4
                  ♡ 10 9 8 5
                  ◇ 8 6
                  ♣ J 7 3
♠ Q 3 2                              ♠ K 6
♡ 6 4              N                 ♡ A K Q
◇ 7 5 3        W       E             ◇ A K Q J 10
♣ K 8 6 5 4                          ♣ A 9 2
                   S
                  ♠ J 10 9 5
                  ♡ J 7 3 2
                  ◇ 9 4 2
                  ♣ Q 10
```

WEST	NORTH	EAST	SOUTH
		2♣	No
2◇	No	3NT	No
4NT	No	6◇	All pass

With support and a ruffing value, West naturally passed 6◇.
There are eleven obvious tricks. Where is the twelfth?

There are three chances: (1) ♠A singleton as long as you first
lead low through the player with the ♠A.

(2) North has ♠A doubleton. West leads a low spade. If North
ducks, ♠K wins. Duck the next spade. If ♠A drops, 6◇ is home.

(3) North has the ♠A and three or more clubs.

♠A singleton is a 1% shot and doubleton ♠A with North is 2%.
The third option is best. Take the ♡A, draw two rounds of trumps,
cash the ♡K and ruff the ♡Q in hand. Now lead a low spade. If
North plays the ♠A, the rest is easy.

If North ducks the spade, your ♠K wins. Now play the rest of
the trumps, discarding three clubs from hand. Everyone is down
to four cards. You have ♠Q-3 ♣K-8 in hand and ♠6 ♣A-9-2 in
dummy. If the situation is as hoped and North has not discarded
a club, the ♠A will be bare. Play a low spade from both hands,
setting up the ♠Q. If North has discarded a club, you must
decide whether clubs were originally 3-2 or 4-1. As 3-2 is more
likely, play a club to the king and a club to the ace. If you are
right, dummy's last club will be high.

56. You, East, hold:

```
♠ K 7 3        Dealer West : Nil vulnerable
♡ A J 5        WEST    NORTH    EAST    SOUTH
◇ K 4          1◇      No       2♣      No
♣ Q J 6 5 3    2♡      No       ?
```

How should East continue?

Answer: For 2♡, you can expect 16+ points and normally at least five diamonds and four hearts. Clearly you have enough for game but to jump to 3NT would be hasty. With slam feasible, your best move is 2♠, fourth-suit forcing to see what further information you can glean from partner.

```
♠ K 7 3        WEST    NORTH    EAST    SOUTH
♡ A J 5        1◇      No       2♣      No
◇ K 4          2♡      No       2♠      No
♣ Q J 6 5 3    2NT     No       ?
```

What do you do now?

Answer: 2NT shows at least one stopper in spades but is ambivalent as to strength. As you responded at the two-level, partner's 2♡ reverse was forcing to game. With spades doubly stopped and no fit for clubs, partner might have jumped to 3NT if minimum, perhaps with a 3-4-5-1 pattern. 2NT may have extra strength or may have just one stopper in spades and be happy to hear some suggestion from you other than no-trumps. At this stage your best move is 4NT, inviting 6NT.

```
♠ A 4                      ♠ K 7 3
♡ Q 10 9 2                 ♡ A J 5
◇ A Q J 10 2               ◇ K 4
♣ A 7                      ♣ Q J 6 5 3
```

Encouraged by the ace in your suit, West accepted the invitation and bid 6NT. North leads the five of spades. If you play low from dummy, South produces the jack. Plan the play for West.

```
              ♠ 10 8 6 5
              ♡ 8 4
              ◇ 9 6 5
              ♣ K 10 8 4
♠ A 4                            ♠ K 7 3
♡ Q 10 9 2                       ♡ A J 5
◇ A Q J 10 2    W  E             ◇ K 4
♣ A 7                            ♣ Q J 6 5 3
              ♠ Q J 9 2
              ♡ K 7 6 3
              ◇ 8 7 3
              ♣ 9 2
```

WEST	NORTH	EAST	SOUTH
1◇	No	2♣	No
2♡	No	2♠	No
2NT	No	4NT	No
6NT	No	No	No

You have nine tricks on top. With the ♡K onside you have two extra heart tricks and can concede a club. If the ♣K is onside, you can score two extra tricks in hearts even if you have to lose one. Therefore, since you are home if either of the missing kings is onside, assume they are both wrong. Can you still cope then?

There is an additional chance, a 3-3 break in clubs. Therefore tackle clubs first. However to take the ♠K and run the ♣Q is not best. Should North win and shift to a heart, you will have to choose between finessing in hearts or playing for clubs 3-3.

A better plan is to win the first trick in hand and lead the ♣7. If North has the ♣K and plays it, the rest of the clubs are likely to be high. If North has the ♣K and plays low, dummy wins and you can now set up the extra tricks you need by playing on hearts.

If South wins the club, you will have time to test the clubs first. If they do not break, you can fall back on the heart finesse.

Harold Franklin, one of Britain's best players and later Chief Tournament Director of the World Bridge Federation, was declarer on this deal and made comfortably by leading the ♣7 at trick two.

57. You, West, hold:

♠ K Q J 9 6 4   Dealer East : Both vulnerable
♡ A Q 6   WEST   NORTH   EAST   SOUTH
♢ 7 5   1NT   No
♣ K Q   ?

What should West respond?

Answer: You have chances for slam (♡K, ♢A, and ♣A-x-x or longer with partner would be enough to make slam odds-on) but not enough to insist on slam. Start by jumping to 3♠.

If you play transfers, the jump to 3♠ is still suitable to show a one-suiter with slam potential. If you transfer to spades, how would you continue after opener bids 2♠?

♠ K Q J 9 6 4   WEST   NORTH   EAST   SOUTH
♡ A Q 6   1NT   No
♢ 7 5   3♠   No   4♣   No
♣ K Q   ?

What next?

Answer: Over 3♠, 3NT would have shown only a doubleton in spades and 4♠ would have been spade support but with a weak opening. 4♣ is a cue-bid showing spade support, a maximum 1NT and the ace of clubs. The ♣A is one of the useful cards for slam and the maximum 1NT is a boon, too. Bid 4♡ to show the ♡A. The diamonds are still a worry. Partner could have 14 HCP without the ace or king of diamonds. You will need to be satisfied that you are not missing the top diamonds before committing to the small slam.

♠ K Q J 9 6 4   ♠ A 7 3 2
♡ A Q 6   ♡ J 7 2
♢ 7 5   ♢ K Q 6
♣ K Q   ♣ A 8 4

You eventually arrive in 6♠ and North leads the jack of clubs. How would you plan the play?

```
            ♠ 10 5
            ♡ K 4 3
            ◇ A 9 3
            ♣ J 10 9 5 2
♠ K Q J 9 6 4                    ♠ A 7 3 2
♡ A Q 6          N               ♡ J 7 2
◇ 7 5        W       E           ◇ K Q 6
♣ K Q           S               ♣ A 8 4
            ♠ 8
            ♡ 10 9 8 5
            ◇ J 10 8 4 2
            ♣ 7 6 3
```

WEST	NORTH	EAST	SOUTH
		1NT	No
3♠	No	4♣	No
4♡	No	4NT	No
5♠	No	6♠	All pass

Normally a 1NT (or 2NT) opener is not permitted to bid beyond game to initiate a slam auction but after West's 4♡, showing the ♡A but denying the ◇A, East is entitled to take control of the bidding. West has shown slam interest already and East has a strong holding in diamonds. West's 5♠ reply to Roman Key Card Blackwood showed two key cards (the ♠K and ♡A) plus the queen of trumps.

Had East bid 4♠ over 4♡, West might have continued with 5♣, showing second-round club control. That clearly makes diamonds the focal point and East should then jump to 6♠.

You have a potential loser in each red suit. Win the lead in hand, draw trumps, cash your other club winner and then lead a diamond. If North has the ◇A and takes it, you can discard two heart losers on the third diamond and third club. If North has the ◇A and plays low, dummy wins and you discard your other diamond on the ♣A. You lose just one heart.

If South has the ◇A, you will need South to hold the ♡K, too. 6♠ fails only when North has ♡K and South ◇A.

58. You, West, hold:

♠ A Q 9 7 6	Dealer West : Both vulnerable			
♡ K 3	WEST	NORTH	EAST	SOUTH
◇ A Q 9	1♠	No	2♣	No
♣ A 5 4	?			

What should West rebid?

Answer: One structure has 2NT as 15-17 and 3NT as 18-19. The advantage of this approach is that it narrows opener's range but the drawback is that it consumes considerable bidding space, which might be useful for slam exploration.

The other popular approach is to rebid 2NT with 15-19, leaving responder room to make a descriptive rebid below game level. 2NT here would also allow partner to show three-card spade support. To jump to 3NT may end the auction with 4♠ on a 5-3 fit being the superior contract.

In either method, opener's 2NT rebid is forcing, as it shows at least 15 points opposite a two-over-one response.

♠ A Q 9 7 6	WEST	NORTH	EAST	SOUTH
♡ K 3	1♠	No	2♣	No
◇ A Q 9	2NT	No	3♠	No
♣ A 5 4	?			

What now?

Answer: 3♠ shows three or more spades but does not promise extra strength. However, East may have extra values. Bid 4♣ as a cue-bid to show the ace of clubs plus slam interest. If partner then bids 4♠, you may be high enough

♠ A Q 9 7 6		♠ K 8 5 2
♡ K 3	N	♡ A J 7
◇ A Q 9	W E	◇ 5 4 2
♣ A 5 4	S	♣ K Q 3

You have arrived in 6♠ and North starts with the jack of clubs. How would you plan the play?

```
              ♠ J 4
              ♡ 10 2
              ◇ K 10 6 3
              ♣ J 10 9 8 7

♠ A Q 9 7 6                      ♠ K 8 5 2
♡ K 3              N             ♡ A J 7
◇ A Q 9        W       E         ◇ 5 4 2
♣ A 5 4                          ♣ K Q 3
                  S
              ♠ 10 3
              ♡ Q 9 8 6 5 4
              ◇ J 8 7
              ♣ 6 2
```

WEST	NORTH	EAST	SOUTH
1♠	No	2♣	No
2NT	No	3♠	No
4♣	No	4♡	No
4NT	No	5♡	No
6♠	No	No	No

4♡ over 4♣ showed the ♡A and in this context also promised
values with slam potential. 5♡ in reply to 4NT Roman Key Card
Blackwood showed two key cards, the ♡A and ♠K.

As East manufactured the 2♣ response in order to make a
delayed game raise, East might well have continued with 4♠
over 2NT (or over 3NT) to show this hand type. West would
still have asked with 4NT and bid the slam.

Win the lead and start on trumps by cashing the ♠K first.
This guards against South's holding all four missing spades.
Draw trumps, cash the ♡K, ♡A and ruff the ♡J. Then play off
your club winners, ending in dummy.

At this point you have trumps in each hand and you and dummy
have a void in hearts and a void in clubs. Lead a diamond from
dummy. If South follows low, play your ◇9. North wins but has to
lead a diamond into your tenace or concede a ruff-and-discard.

If South plays the ◇J on dummy's diamond, cover with the
◇Q. North wins but is again faced with the same losing options.

59. You, West, hold:

	Dealer South : Both vulnerable			
♠ 8 3		WEST	NORTH	EAST	SOUTH
♡ A J 10 9 7					No
◇ A 7 2		1♡	No	2◇	No
♣ A Q 5		?			

What should West rebid?

Answer: With 15 HCP, including three aces, you are too strong for 2♡, which can be passed. The same applies to 3◇. A rebid of 2NT showing 15+ points would be forcing but the weakness in spades is a concern. Given that neither opponent has bid spades, 2NT would be a reasonable risk if there were no better action.

Best is 3♣, a strong rebid as it is beyond two of the suit opened. 3♣ is safe. If clubs are raised, you can always revert to diamonds.

	WEST	NORTH	EAST	SOUTH
♠ 8 3				No
♡ A J 10 9 7	1♡	No	2◇	No
◇ A 7 2	3♣	No	3♡	No
♣ A Q 5	?			

What now?

Answer: 3♡ shows three-card support and may be a very strong hand. As you are minimum, you might wish to sign off in 4♡ but your ◇A makes a slam try reasonable. If partner has ◇K-Q-J-x-x plus the ♠A and a heart honour, 6♡ should be no worse than 50%. Bid 4♣, a cue-bid showing the ♣A and denying the ♠A.

♠ 8 3		♠ Q 10 6
♡ A J 10 9 7		♡ K 8 2
◇ A 7 2		◇ K Q 4 3
♣ A Q 5		♣ 9 4 2

East bids 4♡ over 4♣ and you pass. North leads the ♠7. The ♠10 loses to the jack and South continues with ♠K and ♠A. North follows as you ruff the third round. How do you continue?

125

```
              ♠ 9 7 5 2
              ♡ Q 6 5
              ◇ J 10
              ♣ J 10 7 6
♠ 8 3                              ♠ Q 10 6
♡ A J 10 9 7                       ♡ K 8 2
◇ A 7 2           N                ◇ K Q 4 3
♣ A Q 5        W     E             ♣ 9 4 2
                  S
              ♠ A K J 4
              ♡ 4 3
              ◇ 9 8 6 5
              ♣ K 8 3
```

Partner's hand is a disappointment, but the longer you play, the less you will be surprised by anything that partners produce. As your 3♣ promised five hearts, East should bid 4♡ over 3♣ to show three-card support in a weak hand.

You have already lost two tricks and may still lose a heart and two clubs. On the optimistic side, the club finesse might be on, diamonds could be 3-3 (allowing you to discard a club) and you may not have a heart loser if you can find the queen.

You could finesse either way in hearts but the normal play with this combination is to cash ♡K and then finesse against South. This wins if the ♡Q is singleton in either hand or if South holds two, three or four hearts including the queen. As you have a solid trump sequence, you can afford to lead the ♡J from hand to tempt a cover by North. If North follows low, you can still rise with the ♡K and run the ♡8 next.

Your best move is to delay trumps and test the club finesse first. Cross to dummy with a diamond and lead a low club to the queen. If that loses, play hearts in the normal way as above.

If the ♣Q wins, South has turned up with the ♣K as well as the A-K-J in spades. That makes 11 HCP and as South passed as dealer, North will hold the ♡Q. In that case, lead the ♡J for a first-round finesse in hearts. This wins on the actual layout above but also caters for North holding four trumps to the queen.

60. You, East, hold:

♠ Q 6   Dealer West : North-South vulnerable
♡ 7 3   WEST   NORTH   EAST   SOUTH
◇ A K Q   1♡   No   ?
♣ K Q 8 7 3 2

What would you respond with the East cards?

Answer: A jump-shift to 3♣ is permissible with 16 HCP but that does not mean it is obligatory. Your clubs are all right but are nothing special. If you do jump to 3♣ and partner bids 3♡, you are not well-placed for your next action. A simple two-over-one 2♣ is adequate. If partner rebids 2♡, you can sensibly continue with 3◇ to focus on the spade problem for 3NT.

♠ Q 6   Dealer West : North-South vulnerable
♡ 7 3   WEST   NORTH   EAST   SOUTH
◇ A K Q   1♡   No   2♣   No
♣ K Q 8 7 3 2 3♡   No   ?

What now?

Answer: An opening hand opposite an opening hand makes game a reasonable chance. An opening hand opposite an opener who can jump-rebid makes slam probable as long as a trump fit exists. In this context, you have a very powerful hand. With opener promising at least six hearts, a trump fit exists and your best continuation is 4NT. If you play Roman Key Card Blackwood, this asks for key cards based on the agreed trump suit or, if no trump suit has been explicity agreed, as in this auction, it asks for key cards based on the last bid suit.

♠ K 10   ♠ Q 6
♡ A K 9 8 6 5 4   ♡ 7 3
◇ J 10   ◇ A K Q
♣ A 4   ♣ K Q 8 7 3 2

Against 6♡, North leads ♡Q, taken by the ♡A. When the ♡K is cashed, South discards the ◇2. Plan West's play.

```
                    ♠ J 9 7 5 3
                    ♡ Q J 10
                    ◇ 9
                    ♣ J 10 6 5
    ♠ K 10                              ♠ Q 6
    ♡ A K 9 8 6 5 4    N               ♡ 7 3
    ◇ J 10          W      E            ◇ A K Q
    ♣ A 4              S                ♣ K Q 8 7 3 2
                    ♠ A 8 4 2
                    ♡ 2
                    ◇ 8 7 6 5 4 3 2
                    ♣ 9
```

WEST	NORTH	EAST	SOUTH
1♡	No	2♣	No
3♡	No	4NT	No
5♣	No	5◇	No
6♡	No	No	No

5♣ showed 0 or 3 key cards, clearly three (♡A-K and ♣A). 5◇ asked for the trump queen. 5♡ would deny the ♡Q and East would have passed that. West knew from the 5◇ ask that two key cards were not missing (else East would sign off in 5♡) and with an extra trump, West elected to jump to the slam.

6♡ would make with trumps 2-2. When they turn out to be 3-1, be grateful North did not lead a spade. You now need to discard your spades. You can pitch one on the third diamond and one on the third club, or discard both losers on the clubs.

In both cases you need North to follow to at least two rounds of clubs. Therefore start the clubs first. If both opponents follow to two clubs, cash your three diamonds next and then the third club.

When South shows out on the second club, ruff a club and return to dummy with a diamond. Cash the ♣Q, discarding one spade, and pitch the other spade on the fifth club. North ruffs but it is too late. It would be unlucky to fail because North is short in diamonds but since the slam cannot be made if North does not have two clubs, it costs nothing to test the clubs first.

61. You, West, hold:

♠ A K J 10 8 4   Dealer West : Nil vulnerable
♡ A Q 5   WEST   NORTH   EAST   SOUTH
♢ 9 4   ?
♣ K 2

What would you open with the West cards?

Answer: There are only five losers but this hand is not strong enough to justify an Acol 2♠ opening or a Benjamin 2♣ opening. It is sensible to play these as having 8½-9 playing tricks. If you have eight tricks, partner needs 1½-2 tricks to make game reasonable, but with as much as that, partner will respond to a 1-opening. You should open 1♠.

♠ A K J 10 8 4   Dealer West : Nil vulnerable
♡ A Q 5   WEST   NORTH   EAST   SOUTH
♢ 9 4   1♠   No   1NT   No
♣ K 2   ?

What do you bid now?

Answer: You can expect about 6-9 points for the 1NT response, occasionally 5 points or 10. You have 17 HCP. Counting two extra points (either for the length in spades or for the two doubletons, since your spades are self-sufficient) brings you to 19 total points and that is enough to try for game. Bid 4♠.

Another way to look at it is that you have five losers and a 1NT response will usually produce two tricks. That will reduce your losers to three, enough to justify bidding for ten tricks when your trump suit is so strong.

♠ A K J 10 8 4   ♠ 9 3
♡ A Q 5   ♡ 8 6 4
♢ 9 4   ♢ J 6 2
♣ K 2   ♣ A Q J 6 4

Against 4♠, North leads the ♢A, ♢K and a third diamond to South's ♢Q. How do you plan the play?

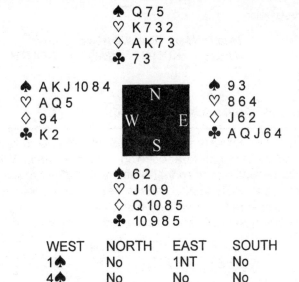

```
                    ♠ Q 7 5
                    ♡ K 7 3 2
                    ◇ A K 7 3
                    ♣ 7 3
    ♠ A K J 10 8 4        N        ♠ 9 3
    ♡ A Q 5                        ♡ 8 6 4
    ◇ 9 4          W        E      ◇ J 6 2
    ♣ K 2                          ♣ A Q J 6 4
                       S
                    ♠ 6 2
                    ♡ J 10 9
                    ◇ Q 10 8 5
                    ♣ 10 9 8 5
```

WEST	NORTH	EAST	SOUTH
1♠	No	1NT	No
4♠	No	No	No

After ruffing the third diamond, do not be tempted to play a club to dummy's jack or queen in order to lead the ♠9 for a first-round finesse. That would be fine if South had ♠Q-x-x or even ♠Q-x-x-x, and you might even score an overtrick then.

However, as your aim is to make the contract and overtricks are of no concern, crossing to dummy for a spade finesse is far from safe. When the finesse loses, you are in severe jeopardy. If the layout is as above, North can win with the ♠Q and return a club. Now you will probably be two down.

There is an easy solution and the spade finesse is merely a red herring, as is the heart finesse. At trick 4, play the spades from the top. If the ♠Q falls singleton or doubleton you make eleven tricks. If the ♠Q has not fallen in two rounds, continue spades. Win any return and draw the last trump if they were originally 4-1. Then run the clubs to discard your two hearts from hand.

It would be an error to abandon trumps after ♠A and ♠K and start on clubs. North can ruff the third club and you are left with a heart loser if North exits with the fourth diamond. There is a simple principle here. If dummy has a long, running suit but no outside entry, remove all the trumps before running that suit.

62. You, West, hold:

♠ A K 4   Dealer West : East-West vulnerable
♡ Q 10 6   WEST   NORTH   EAST   SOUTH
◇ A Q J 2   ?
♣ A K 5

What would you open with the West cards?

Answer: The standard approach for balanced hands is to open 2NT with 20-22 points and to use 2♣ for stronger hands. With 23-24 points, most prefer to open 2♣ and rebid 2NT after a 2◇ negative response. Bidding after opener's 2NT rebid follows the same paths as after a 2NT opening.

With more than 24 HCP and a balanced hand, some rebid 3NT (25-28 points), 4NT (29-30) or 5NT (31-32). A useful alternative after 2♣ : 2◇ is to bid 2NT with 23-24 balanced and to use an artificial 2♡ rebid to force to game (2♣ : 2◇, 2♡). Over this 2♡, 2♠ operates as a second negative and now opener's 2NT rebid is forcing, with 25+ points and a balanced hand. This is a wide-ranging rebid and gives the partnership more room to explore the best contract. One huge benefit is that responder can rebid over this 2NT as after a 2NT opening. This is more efficient than responder's actions after opener rebids 3NT with 25+ balanced.

Quite a good scheme after 2♣ : 2◇ is to use three-level rebids as powerful one-suiters, around the 19-22 HCP mark but not forcing, 2♠ as a game-force with 5+ spades and 2♡ as the artificial game-force, denying 5+ spades. That telescopes the hand types for the Benjamin 2♣ and 2◇ openings into one opening bid.

East has little but enough to rebid 3NT after 2♣ : 2◇, 2NT. North leads the ♡4 to South's king. How do you plan the play?

```
                    ♠ 10 3
                    ♡ A 9 8 4 3
                    ◇ 7 6
                    ♣ Q J 8 4
    ♠ A K 4                              ♠ Q 7 2
    ♡ Q 10 6          N                  ♡ J 5 2
    ◇ A Q J 2    W         E             ◇ 8 5 3
    ♣ A K 5                              ♣ 7 6 3 2
                        S
                    ♠ J 9 8 6 5
                    ♡ K 7
                    ◇ K 10 9 4
                    ♣ 10 9
```

WEST	NORTH	EAST	SOUTH
2♣	No	2◇	No
2NT	No	3NT	All pass

The danger in many a hand is to play mechanically,
particularly to trick one, and then it may be too late to undo the
wrong. In no-trumps it is sound technique to start by counting
your certain winners. Here you have five top tricks in the black
suits. The ◇A brings your tally to six. You will be able to make
one trick from the hearts and still need two more. The two extra
tricks need to come from the diamonds.

If diamonds are 3-3, the contract is secure if South has the
◇K or the hearts break 4-3. If hearts are 5-2, you need South
to hold the ◇K, else North will have an entry to the established
hearts. The odds for diamonds 3-3 are much worse than 50%,
while playing for South to have the ◇K is a 50% chance.

It may seem that you need South to hold ◇K-doubleton, as
you have only one entry to dummy to take the diamond finesse.
As North has probably led from a long suit, it is quite likely that
North has the ♡A. That will give you a second entry to dummy
but only if you jettison the ♡Q under South's king at trick one.

Now, as the cards lie, no matter how the opponents defend,
the ♡J is an entry to dummy for one diamond finesse and the
♠Q is another. With diamonds 4-2, the limit is nine tricks.

63. You, West, hold:

♠ A Q J 7 6 5   Dealer East : East-West vulnerable
♡ A   WEST   NORTH   EAST   SOUTH
♢ 4   No   1NT*
♣ A Q 10 7 4   ?
                      *12-14

What action would you take as West?

Answer: You have a powerful spade suit, exceptionally good shape and only three losers. Opposite as little as ♣J-x-x and a couple of spades, game is a reasonable prospect. To bid less than game shows extreme vitamin deficiency. The sensible, practical choice is 4♠. The alternative is 2NT, forcing to game and showing a powerful two-suiter, at least 5-5. The 2NT bid leaves open the possibility of slam opposite some useful values like ♣K and ♢A, not impossible on the bidding.

The deal arose in the 1989 world teams semi-finals. In the Bermuda Bowl (open teams), the USA West bid 1♠ over 1♣ and played it there for +170. A vulnerable game gone begging. Brazil's East-West also stopped out of game. Poland reached 4♠ via a strong, artificial sequence, showing a black two-suiter, and Australia followed the recommended (1NT) : 4♠ path.

In the Venice Cup (women's teams), three pairs reached game, one after South passed. The USA East-West had a handy gadget for the West cards:

WEST	NORTH	EAST	SOUTH
		No	1NT*
3♣ (1)	No	3♠	No
4♠	No	No	No

(1) Five or more spades plus long clubs

♠ A Q J 7 6 5   ♠ 10 8
♡ A   ♡ 10 8 7 6 5 2
♢ 4   ♢ A 10 8 7
♣ A Q 10 7 4   ♣ 6

Bidding 4♠ is one thing. Making it is another.
North leads the ♢3. How would you plan the play?

```
                    ♠ 2
                    ♡ J 9 3
                    ◇ Q 9 6 3 2
                    ♣ K J 8 3

♠ A Q J 7 6 5                        ♠ 10 8
♡ A              ┌─────────┐        ♡ 10 8 7 6 5 2
◇ 4              │   N     │        ◇ A 10 8 7
♣ A Q 10 7 4     │ W     E │        ♣ 6
                 │   S     │
                 └─────────┘
                    ♠ K 9 4 3
                    ♡ K Q 4
                    ◇ K J 5
                    ♣ 9 5 2
```

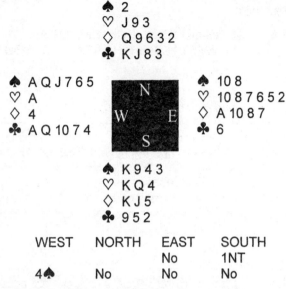

WEST	NORTH	EAST	SOUTH
		No	1NT
4♠	No	No	No

The ◇3 lead means diamonds are 4-4 or 5-3. Therefore you can ruff three red cards safely in your own hand to score your three low trumps. That guarantees five spade tricks. Add the three outside aces and you have eight tricks. Two club ruffs in dummy and the tally is ten. The third club will be ruffed with the ♠10. If it happens to be over-ruffed you lose a club ruff but your spade tricks in hand rise to six.

What does all this tell you about the line of play to adopt? Firstly, you do not need the club finesse. Secondly, do not play too quickly to trick 2. If you go for the club ruffs first, you can score only two red suit ruffs. The right order is ◇A, ruff a diamond, cash the ♡A and ♣A, ruff a club with the ♠8, ruff another diamond, ruff a club with the ♠10. All have followed so far and you are well-placed.

Ruff a heart with the ♠7 and exit with a club. North wins and plays a red card, which you ruff with the ♠J. South is down to spades only. Exit with your last club. South ruffs and leads a low spade. You finesse the ♠Q, knowing it will win since you have been counting North's points. You make eleven tricks for +650. In the Bermuda Bowl, the two declarers in 4♠ failed.

64. You, West, hold:

♠ 7 5 3   Dealer West : Both vulnerable
♡ A K Q J 10 5 3   WEST   NORTH   EAST   SOUTH
◇ A   ?
♣ A K

What would you open with the West cards?

Answer: Although you have only 21 HCP, there are ten winners with hearts as trumps. This is enough to open 2♣.

♠ 7 5 3   Dealer West : Both vulnerable
♡ A K Q J 10 5 3   WEST   NORTH   EAST   SOUTH
◇ A   2♣   No   3◇   No
♣ A K   ?

The 3◇ is a positive reply with 5+ diamonds. What now?

Answer: There is nothing wrong with a 3♡ rebid but a useful agreement is to play a jump-rebid by the 2♣ opener to show a solid suit and thereby set trumps. With such an agreement, you rebid 4♡. Naturally the bid is forcing after a positive reply.

♠ 7 5 3   Dealer West : Both vulnerable
♡ A K Q J 10 5 3   WEST   NORTH   EAST   SOUTH
◇ A   2♣   No   3◇   No
♣ A K   4♡   No   4♠   No
      ?

What is 4♠? What do you do next?

Answer: 4♠ is a cue-bid and 4NT next is a sensible move. After 5◇, one ace, rebid 5NT to show all the aces are held.

♠ 7 5 3   ♠ A 4
♡ A K Q J 10 5 3   ♡ 4
◇ A   ◇ K 8 6 4 3
♣ A K   ♣ 7 5 4 3 2

You end in 6♡. North leads the ♠K. Plan your play.

```
                    ♠ K Q J 8
                    ♡ 2
                    ◇ 7 5 2
                    ♣ Q J 9 8 6
  ♠ 7 5 3                              ♠ A 4
  ♡ A K Q J 10 5 3        N            ♡ 4
  ◇ A                 W        E       ◇ K 8 6 4 3
  ♣ A K                                ♣ 7 5 4 3 2
                         S
                    ♠ 10 9 6 2
                    ♡ 9 8 7 6
                    ◇ Q J 10 9
                    ♣ 10
```

WEST	NORTH	EAST	SOUTH
2♣	No	3◇	No
4♡	No	4♠	No
5♣	No	5♡	No
6♣	No	6♡	All pass

Popularly believed to be the best Acol system partnership of all time, the Sharples twins, Bob and Jim, were the ideal third pair for any British team. Their accuracy in bidding was remarkable. In the above auction all the bids after 4♡ were cue-bids with West trying to locate enough values opposite for a grand slam in hearts. Once East could not cue-bid 5♠ over 5♣, there was little hope for 7♡. West might well bid 4NT over 4♠ and follow up with 5NT over 5◇. If East showed two kings, West would bid 7NT while opposite one king, 6♡ is enough.

. The ♠K was led. West was Jim Sharples, who could see twelve tricks, seven in trumps the ♠A, and the A-K in the minor suits. The problem was the blockage in diamonds.

Problem? No problem. Jim's solution was simple and effective: he ducked the ♠K. Whatever North played next, declarer had the answer. Another spade, perhaps? Dummy's ace wins, a diamond to the ace is followed by a spade ruff for the twelfth trick. If North shifts to another suit, declarer wins, draws trumps, unblocks the ◇A and the ♠A is the entry to the ◇K.

65. You, West, hold:

♠ 8	Dealer West : Both vulnerable			
♡ A K 10 9 4 3	WEST	NORTH	EAST	SOUTH
◇ K 10 5	1♡	No	1♠	No
♣ K J 6	?			

What would you rebid with the West cards?

Answer: The choice is between 2♡, showing a minimum opening, normally with 6+ hearts, or 3♡, showing a strong opening and guaranteeing 6+ hearts. On the negative side you have only 14 HCP and partner might expect a bit more. Also the singleton in partner's suit does not enhance your values.

On the other hand your long suit is excellent and you have no wasted high cards. The two red tens are also plus values. With a close decision whether to bid more or less, it is usually better to take the optimistic path.

Another way to look at the West hand: if you replaced any one of the kings with a low card, you would still open 1♡ and rebid 2♡ over 1♠. With a king more than a minimum, it is reasonable, although not mandatory, to make the 3♡ jump-rebid.

What would you do if partner then bids 3♠?

Answer: A rebid of 3NT would be your best bet. The 3♠ rebid suggests partner has a singleton or void in hearts.

What if partner had rebid 4♣ or 4◇ over 3♡?

Answer: Although responder could be 6-5 and 4♣ or 4◇ is natural, it is more practical to play a new suit after opener's jump-rebid as a cue-bid, agreeing opener's suit as trumps.

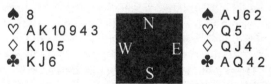

♠ 8 ♠ A J 6 2
♡ A K 10 9 4 3 ♡ Q 5
◇ K 10 5 ◇ Q J 4
♣ K J 6 ♣ A Q 4 2

You end in 6♡. North leads the ◇6 to South's ace. The ◇2 is returned and North plays the ◇3. Plan your play.

137

```
           ♠ Q 10 7 5 3
           ♡ 7
           ◇ 9 8 7 6 3
           ♣ 10 7
♠ 8                            ♠ A J 6 2
♡ A K 10 9 4 3      N         ♡ Q 5
◇ K 10 5        W       E     ◇ Q J 4
♣ K J 6              S         ♣ A Q 4 2
           ♠ K 9 4
           ♡ J 8 6 2
           ◇ A 2
           ♣ 9 8 5 3
```

WEST	NORTH	EAST	SOUTH
1♡	No	1♠	No
3♡	No	4NT	No
5♡	No	6♡	All pass

4NT was Roman Key Card Blackwood, based on hearts, and 5♡ showed two key cards but no ♡Q. With one key card missing, East settles for 6♡.

The deal arose in the European Teams Championship in Torquay in 1962. Victory went to the British Open Team and here West was Tony Priday and East, Alan Truscott. The original bidding sequence has been lost but West was in 6♡.

Tony won the second diamond in hand with the king and immediately played a spade to the ace and ruffed a spade. Next came the ♡A and a heart to the queen. Had trumps been 3-2, he could return to hand with a club to draw the last trump.

When trumps were 4-1, another spade was ruffed to reduce declarer's trump length to the same as South's. Next came the clubs and fortunately South had at least three of them. On the fourth club, Tony discarded the ◇10. At trick twelve the lead was in dummy. The diamond was led, South had to ruff and West over-ruffed. Contract made.

Note West's early play of the ♠A and spade ruff to shorten his trumps just in case the hearts did turn out to be 4-1.

66. You, West, hold:

♠ A Q 10 9 4   Dealer West : Both vulnerable
♡ A Q J 10 9 3   WEST   NORTH   EAST   SOUTH
♢ 5   ?
♣ K

What would you open with the West cards?

Answer: Although the hand has only four losers, this hand pattern is not attractive for an Acol Two opening or for a Benjamin 2♣ opening, showing around nine playing tricks. If you start with such an opening, it is almost impossible to describe the freakish nature of your hand.

With a 6-5 pattern it is normal to start with the 6-card suit, then show the 5-card suit and, if no fit has been found yet, repeat the 5-card suit if that is convenient. Start with 1♡. If the bidding happens to go 1♡ : 2♣, 2♠ : 3NT it would be unwise to bid 4♠. Rather rebid 4♡.

♠ A Q 10 9 4   Dealer West : Both vulnerable
♡ A Q J 10 9 3   WEST   NORTH   EAST   SOUTH
♢ 5   1♡   No   2♡   No
♣ K   ?

What now?

Answer: For slam to be a good bet, partner needs three of the four critical cards, ♠K, ♡K, ♢A, ♣A. As that would give partner 10 HCP at least, it is highly unlikely to find that within a 2♡ response. If partner has any less, slam will be at best on a finesse. Be satisfied with 4♡.

♠ A Q 10 9 4   ♠ 7 5 2
♡ A Q J 10 9 3   ♡ 8 6 5 2
♢ 5   ♢ J 10
♣ K   ♣ A 7 6 5

You are in 6♡ after a wild 2♡ : 3♡, 6♡ sequence. The ♢A is led, followed by the ♢3 to South's ♢Q. Plan the play.

```
           ♠ 8 6
           ♡ K
           ◊ A 9 7 6 3 2
           ♣ J 9 4 2

♠ A Q 10 9 4                    ♠ 7 5 2
♡ A Q J 10 9 3                  ♡ 8 6 5 2
◊ 5            N                ◊ J 10
♣ K          W   E              ♣ A 7 6 5
                 S
           ♠ K J 3
           ♡ 7 4
           ◊ K Q 8 4
           ♣ Q 10 8 3
```

6♡ is a terrible slam and if justice prevailed, you would be two down at least. However, all of us have been in terrible slams from time to time. Once there do not wail about the bidding. Your task is to give yourself the best chance of success.

The best chance to avoid a heart loser is to finesse for the king. That entails overtaking the ♣K with the ace. The best chance to avoid a spade loser is to take two finesses in the hope that South has both missing spade honours. This is a much better hope than playing North for a singleton spade honour.

The problem is that if you use the ♣A as an entry to take the heart finesse, you no longer have two entries to dummy to take two spade finesses even if the ♡K is onside. If you play ♣K to the ace and lead a low heart to the queen, winning, and the ♡A then drops the ♡K, you have the ♡8 in dummy as one entry but there is no second entry to dummy.

It is a better chance that the ♡K is singleton in either hand than North having ♠K or ♠J singleton and so you should ruff the diamond with any trump other than the ♡A or ♡3. Next play the ♡A. When the ♡K drops, play the ♡3 to the ♡8 and lead a spade to your ten. When that holds, overtake the ♣K with the ace and take another spade finesse. When both spade finesses work, justice has turned a blind eye. Note that you fail if you ruff the second diamond with the ♡3. You need the ♡3 to cross to the ♡8 as the extra entry to dummy.

67. You, West, hold:

♠ A 2	Dealer East : Both vulnerable			
♡ A 7 5	WEST	NORTH	EAST	SOUTH
◇ 10 7 2			2NT	No
♣ A 9 8 7 6	?			

What would you respond with the West cards?

Answer: If you play 3♣ as '5-Card Major Stayman', that would be your best start in case opener has five hearts. If that is not part of your armoury, you can bid 3♣ anyway (as Stayman or Baron) and continue with 4♣ next. That implies a 5-card suit and slam interest.

♠ A 2	Dealer East : Both vulnerable			
♡ A 7 5	WEST	NORTH	EAST	SOUTH
◇ 10 7 2			2NT	No
♣ A 9 8 7 6	3♣	No	3NT	No
	?			

You are playing 3♣ as '5-card Major Stayman'. What does opener's 3NT reply mean? What do you do now?

Answer: The 3NT reply says, 'No 5-card major, no 4-card major'. You should continue with 4♣, a natural bid showing 5+ clubs and slam interest.

♠ A 2	♠ K Q 8
♡ A 7 5	♡ 6 3 2
◇ 10 7 2	◇ A K Q J
♣ A 9 8 7 6	♣ K Q 3

After 2NT : 3♣, 3NT : 4♣ East should bid 4◇, a cue-bid with club support (4NT instead of a cue-bid would deny three clubs). West continues with 4NT, Roman Key Card Blackwood, and after the 5♠ reply showing two key cards plus the ♣Q, West bids 6♣.

North leads the ♡K. West wins and plays a club to the king. On the ♣Q South discards the ♠3. Plan the play.

```
                   ♠ 9 5
                   ♡ K Q J
                   ◇ 9 6 4 3
                   ♣ J 10 5 4
♠ A 2                                   ♠ K Q 8
♡ A 7 5          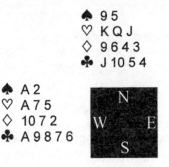   ♡ 6 3 2
◇ 10 7 2                                ◇ A K Q J
♣ A 9 8 7 6                             ♣ K Q 3
                   ♠ J 10 7 6 4 3
                   ♡ 10 9 8 4
                   ◇ 8 5
                   ♣ 2
```

7♣ or 7NT is a respectable grand slam but fails when clubs do not break. 6NT is also a fine spot but a heart lead would doom that. Had trumps been 3-2, declarer would have thirteen tricks in 6♣. When South shows out on the second club, declarer has an inevitable trump loser and even twelve tricks are in jeopardy. West needs to eliminate both heart losers. One can be discarded on the third spade and one on the fourth diamond, but which suit should you try first?

After a third club to the ace the instinctive move is to tackle spades first because you have fewer cards there. However, this is a misguided notion. For the slam to make, North needs to hold three diamonds anyway. If not, North will ruff in early and cash a heart. Therefore you should test the diamonds first.

If the diamonds turn out to be 3-3, do not cash the thirteenth yet. Try for three rounds of spades and if they survive, then play the last diamond.

Most of the time you will survive if you start with the spades but on the layout above, North ruffs the third spade and you are two down. The benefit in trying the diamonds first arises when North has four or five (or six) diamonds. When South shows out on the third diamond, you know it is safe to cash the fourth diamond, to which North must follow. Only then do you start on the spades. Once North has more than three diamonds, you need North to have only two spades, not three.

68. You, West, hold:

♠ 9 7 4 3	Dealer East : North-South vulnerable

	WEST	NORTH	EAST	SOUTH
♠ 9 7 4 3				
♡ K 6 2			2NT	No
◇ A J 8 7 2	?			
♣ 6				

What would you respond with the West cards?

Answer: Your primary task is to check whether there is a 4-4 fit in spades. You should therefore bid 3♣, whether you play that as simple Stayman, 5-Card Major Stayman or Baron.

	WEST	NORTH	EAST	SOUTH
♠ 9 7 4 3				
♡ K 6 2			2NT	No
◇ A J 8 7 2	3♣	Double	Redouble	No
♣ 6	?			

What does North's double mean? What do you understand by partner's redouble?

Answer: North's double is lead-directing, asking South to lead a club. East's redouble is generally played as suggesting that 3♣ redoubled might be the place to play. You can expect partner to have five decent clubs or a very strong 4-card holding.

What action do you take now?

Answer: West should trust partner and pass the redouble. West has no help in clubs but has significant strength outside. With at least one sure entry and not a club void, it is worth passing and playing for a high score. With 28-30 combined high card points you probably have enough to make 3♣ on sheer power.

♠ 9 7 4 3	N	♠ A 2
♡ K 6 2		♡ A Q J 5
◇ A J 8 7 2	W E	◇ K 3
♣ 6	S	♣ A Q 10 7 2

The contract is 3♣ redoubled after the above sequence and North leads the ♡3. How would you plan the play.

```
            ♠ K J 8
            ♡ 10 4 3
            ◇ Q 4
            ♣ K J 5 4 3

♠ 9 7 4 3        N         ♠ A 2
♡ K 6 2                    ♡ A Q J 5
◇ A J 8 7 2   W     E      ◇ K 3
♣ 6              S         ♣ A Q 10 7 2

            ♠ Q 10 6 5
            ♡ 9 8 7
            ◇ 10 9 6 5
            ♣ 9 8
```

WEST	NORTH	EAST	SOUTH
		2NT	No
3♣	Double	Redouble	All pass

To double 2♣ Stayman for the lead, one should have at least a five-card suit, no weaker than K-Q-J-x-x. To double 3♣ for the lead, the suit should not be much weaker than that. Perhaps K-J-10-x-x. Even then you run the risk of opener's redoubling with strong clubs.

Lest you think the double of 3♣ was a beginner's error, North was a multi-international playing in the final of a major teams championship in Australia. West was young expert, Kieran Dyke, who did not make just nine tricks. He collected two redoubled overtricks. Winning the heart lead with the king, he led the ♣6 to the ten in dummy. When that held, he cashed the ♡A and ♡Q, followed by the ◇K and a diamond to the ace.

The ◇Q dropping was handy but not necessary. Dyke continued with the ◇J, ruffed low and over-ruffed with the ♣7. Declarer had won the first seven tricks and continued with ace of spades and another spade. No matter how the opponents defended, declarer was able to make three of the last four tricks. Making 3♣ redoubled with two overtricks was worth +1640 and +17 Imps, as North-South at the other table were one down in 6♡. Nothing like having a bit of fun at the bridge table.